KU-788-848

Acknowledgements

This book has been completed with the help of my wife, Gill, who is still a 'motor-moron' but now understands why!

I also wish to thank Trevor Waterworth for invaluable professional help and advice during his years at Trinity and All Saints College.

This book offers help with games skills and athletics lessons taken by the junior school teacher. It is concerned with the teaching of individual skills and small-sided games, not with the coaching of 'major' games, for example, netball, soccer, etc.

The schemes of work cover the programme of study (general) and (specific) of the PE National Curriculum for games and athletics in key stage 2, years 5 to 6, ages 7 to 11.

Each scheme of work for a year group is preceded by a breakdown of the intended learning outcomes, in terms of skills and decision-making, for each unit of work. This overview is intended to assist longer-term planning of the scheme, to show the progressions inside each unit of work, and help with assessment. Units of work deal with invasion, net and fielding/striking skills and games. The principles of attack and defence, rules and scoring are covered in each unit of the scheme.

Each lesson can be used as a basis for two or three games skills sessions.

Athletics is presented in a series of progressive ideas which are suitable for years 3 to 6, in a spiral structure. The reason for presenting the material in this flexible way is to allow teachers to fit athletics programmes into their overall planning for the National Curriculum.

I hope this book will provide a basis for planning and delivering games and athletics units/lessons for primary, generalist teachers and give help and guidance to PE curriculum leaders concerning schemes of work for the whole of key stage 2 of the National Curriculum.

Contents

The development of games skills in the primary school

A   Key stage one principles

(i)   The focus is on the individual learner. Tasks are matched and modified so that all children achieve success at their own level and have opportunities to improve. This implies that tasks are based on the developmental stage they have reached, taking account of individual physical attributes.

(ii)   The content of lessons should be based on a broad repertoire of skills. It is useful to categorise them into:
● Travelling: footwork skills (running, dodging, jumping, etc).
● Travelling with (eg dribbling, carrying) a piece of equipment.
● Sending away (eg passing, throwing, striking).
● Receiving (eg moving to stop, catch or trap).

(iii)   As well as providing this broad range, each category should contain variety (eg striking with foot, hand and implement, using different sizes of ball, different size and shape of bats and sticks, using different distances, targets, heights, speeds and angles). This allows children to broaden and deepen their skill learning so that the acquisition of new skills can easily be accommodated into their growing experience.

(iv)   This principle has an implication for lesson structure – each lesson should contain some travelling, sending and receiving skills, and involve children in situations where they play alongside each other with a partner, using these skills in games which are teacher-directed. Children will be able to devise their own games based on the skills learned. This process helps to develop understanding of the need for and use of rule structures. It is therefore important to set tasks so that each child can be successful at their own level, focus on effort rather than ability, and make extensive use of co-operation (rather than competition).

B   The learning of skills

There are two types of skill to acquire, both of which require the child to process information just as they would in a reading, writing, science or mathematics context:
● 'closed' skills – skills performed in predictable, unchanging environments (eg rolling a ball towards a stationary target);

● 'open' skills – which take place in constantly changing environments (eg the situations that occur in small-sided team ball games).

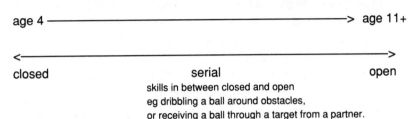

age 4 ——> age 11+

<——>
closed   serial   open
                 skills in between closed and open
                 eg dribbling a ball around obstacles,
                 or receiving a ball through a target from a partner.

Most infant game activities tend towards the closed end of the continuum. It is obvious that a young learner cannot process, memorise and make decisions about masses of complicated information, so keep the teaching points and demonstrations brief.

A different teaching strategy will apply to the more open skill of receiving (stopping, trapping and catching) than to the more closed skill of sending a ball to a stationary target. Receiving requires the child to process information about the sender's action, distance, direction, ball speed and trajectory (flight path), predict where and when the ball will arrive, move the body and hands, foot or implement into the appropriate place and then use the appropriate technique to stop the ball! Sending does not require these complicated anticipatory decisions. Therefore, when teaching an open skill, alert the child to the relevant points (it is useless to know how to hold your hands if you cannot predict where the ball will arrive!) and when teaching a closed skill teach the best way to perform an action.

C   The bridge between key stage 1 and key stage 2

The development of skill in games-like contexts means that children in the 6/7/8 age range can be introduced to activities which begin to bridge the gap between learning skills and applying skills (understanding and decisions) in the context of:
● net-type game situations
● fielding-type game situations
● invading territory-type game situations.

Using skills in a developing context implies:
● that the child can begin to apply skills learned to game-like situations (eg skills learned in maths to attempt investigations, or writing skills to explain a science activity);
● that the child can make anticipatory decisions in a game-like situation based on some understanding of the form or structure of the game being played.

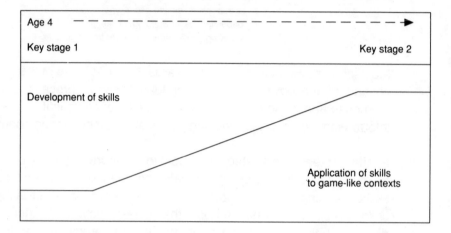

This principle is reflected in the structure of each unit where skills learned, individually or with a partner/group, are applied to game contexts in order to develop knowledge and understanding of the strategies and role structures involved in net-, fielding- and invasion-type games activities.

D   Summary of principles of primary games development

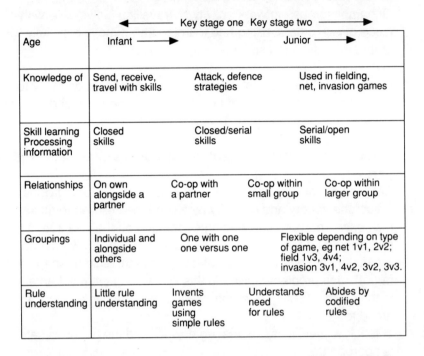

	← Key stage one	Key stage two →	
Age	Infant →	Junior →	
Knowledge of	Send, receive, travel with skills	Attack, defence strategies	Used in fielding, net, invasion games
Skill learning Processing information	Closed skills	Closed/serial skills	Serial/open skills
Relationships	On own alongside a partner	Co-op with a partner	Co-op within small group / Co-op within larger group
Groupings	Individual and alongside others	One with one one versus one	Flexible depending on type of game, eg net 1v1, 2v2; field 1v3, 4v4; invasion 3v1, 4v2, 3v2, 3v3.
Rule understanding	Little rule understanding	Invents games using simple rules	Understands need for rules / Abides by codified rules

The development of a school policy statement and schemes of work are based on these principles of development and planning (see section H 'Planning for the National Curriculum').

A   Lesson structure

(i)   Introductory activity/warm up

Often a vigorous footwork activity or travelling individually with a piece of equipment, using and learning about moving skilfully with others in a restricted space.

The introduction establishes your control. Listening carefully to instructions sets the tone of later activities which demand co-operation and problem-solving.

(ii)   Introduction or development of individual skill or skills with a partner

Set problem-solving tasks which can be modified for individuals. Adjust the variety and difficulty by asking the children to make the task easier or more challenging depending on their degree of success. Ask them: How did they do it? What did they change? (eg distance, speed, the type of ball or bat, the size or shape of the target). Use problem-solving in this way to engage children actively in their own learning, decision-making and evaluation. Don't be afraid to:

● teach a specific technique, eg how to hold the hands to catch, if it is appropriate

● limit the task, eg 'Everyone try dribbling the ball with the inside of their feet.'

Children want to be able to perform a task well. Repeat a practice, emphasise different aspects of the task, set different targets – challenge them!

(iii)   Introduction or development of small group games

Apply the skills learned to game-like situations by:

● Teacher-directed games, where specific strategies and skills are expected to be applied. (Children can be asked to develop their own rule structure, which teaches them about the purpose and need for rules and releases the teacher to intervene in skills teaching.)

● Child-directed games. Give the children some guidance, eg 'Make up a passing game using two cones, two ropes and a ball. Make your game harder when you can play it well.'

Check the safety of their setting out. A variety of solutions will emerge based on the principles you have taught. Intervene to reinforce and deepen learning. Learners should know the purpose of the task and what they are trying to achieve.

(iv) **Concluding activity**
A warm-down activity – return to an individual or partner practice or a choice of one aspect of an individual skill.

The introductory activity-skills practice-game format can be modified for older juniors (9 – 11 years): a modified game can follow the warm-up activities. The skills and decisions being used could be developed in a game context. If the game is breaking down (eg, through inadequate skills, or a lack of successful strategies, or absence of rule structure) you can intervene introducing an appropriate practice before return to the game.

This method is not synonymous with and does not justify a full-sided game of, for example, soccer, netball or rounders.

B **Observation**
The key to successful teaching and learning. Guidance on what to look for or teaching points is given after every skill task and game. This information implies that the teacher knows the criteria involved and is capable of observing these planned criteria or teaching points.

In teaching physical education the observer has to 'video' the action (there is no written evidence!), decide what the child did well andhow to help that individual (or group). This is not an easy task but it is essential to master this teaching strategy in order to assess pupil progress and ensure that each child achieves success.

C **Task-setting and guidance**
Set tasks with clear expectations. Observe the children's performance against your teaching point criteria. Give specific advice on skill technique, eg how to hold the bat or how to process/attend to the appropriate information (eg watch the sender's hand as they release the ball) or strategy.

Demonstration (by pupil or teacher) is a powerful visual aid in conveying a teaching point. Bring pupils round in a semi-circle so all can hear and see. Draw their attention to the important points of the action before the demonstration, and then let them practice the part or whole skill or strategy.

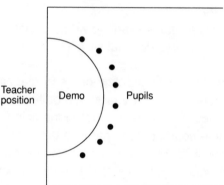

Demonstration can also be used to foster the observation and evaluation skills of pupils. Give positive feedback which tells the child what they have done correctly, then add praise and a further challenge. Always use their name: 'Gurdip, your grip is correct, the arm started straight, and your stance is sideways. That was well done. Can you speed up your arm action next time so that the ball travels further?'

Watch this next attempt and give praise. Giving positive feedback about teaching points and performance criteria lets the child know the correct technique and helps improve performance. Giving value-loaded feedback: 'That's OK, Chris. That was great, Andrew,' confuses because no criteria is used; and giving negative feedback: 'Your throwing stance is hopeless, Ravinder,' destroys confidence.

D   Safety
When helping individuals or teaching groups keep on the outside of the area so that everyone is in view. The corners give the widest angle.

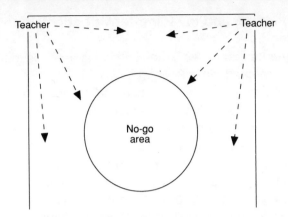

Organise the playing area so that a safe environment is created for playing games. Advice is included in the units on where positioning or use of equipment affects the safety of the skill practice or game.

E   Participation

The guiding principle is that all the children should be involved and active all of the time. For this reason, individual, partner and small-sided games are used throughout each year group scheme.

Relays are not used in this book to teach or practice games skills. A relay activity is defined as one where children are in teams; one child runs, the rest wait in turn.

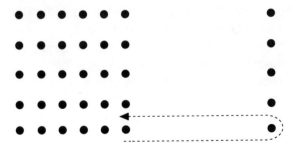

This type of organisation allows five children to participate and 25 to spectate! Relays are often overcompetitive and lead to breakdown of skill and loss of self-esteem for the unsuccessful. They do not help team-work. They are not physical education. The material in this book is designed for maximum participation – the opportunity for all children to gain pleasure and enjoyment through playing games.

F   **Net, fielding and invading-territory decisions and strategies**

Net games (examples of adult versions are volleyball, badminton, tennis) demand the following:
● decisions concerning direction and speed of sending
● decisions concerning movement after sending
● decisions concerning when to send
● awareness of position of partner
● decisions concerning how to defend (moving into line behind the ball, anticipation of direction, trajectory, speed)
● appreciation of changing role between partner in possession (attack) and partner waiting to receive (defence).

Fielding/striking games (adult versions are rounders, cricket, stoolball, softball, baseball) usually played on circular or semi-circular playing areas, demand the following decisions:
● batter: how, when and where to hit the ball
● bowler: how to bowl and on from where the ball will return
● fielders: how to send and receive the ball, where the ball will arrive, where to send it, and how to co-operate as a team.

Invasion games (adult versions are rugby, soccer, netball, hockey, basketball, kabbadi, American football) demand the following:
● development of control
● development of looking around while controlling the ball
● development of signalling for the ball
● development of moving into a space to receive
● development of passing and moving forward
● development of who to pass to, where and when to pass
● development of moving into another team's territory to score
● development of working together as a team.

All types of game share attacking and defensive strategies. These strategies are developed in a progressive way within each year group scheme.

G Progression

The process of physical education, 'Planning; Performing; Evaluating,' is well defined in the PE National Curriculum Non-Strategy Guidance (Section D, 1.0). The progression principles of difficulty and quality are incorporated into all the lesson material.

In this book the progressions used for each year group scheme are reviewed at the start of each year scheme, so that class teachers can relate them to the specific programme of study for key stage 2 games when planning units and lessons. Curriculum leaders can use them to monitor that the schemes cover the general programme of study and end of key stage statements that will be the basis of assessment.

Invasion game progressions embody the principle of using unequal sides (before equal sides) to encourage the attackers to succeed.

Even-sided games, if introduced too early in the learning process, lead to stalemate and a freeze on decision-making because everyone is guarded. Larger sides (eg six versus six) only increase this problem (ie a person in possession has five possible targets, all marked by defenders and all screaming for the ball!).

Teach attacking strategies before defensive strategies. Though it is obvious that the two complement each other, the focus for the skill practices will be either attack or defence, then both.

Defensive strategies begin with marking a player in possession and progress to person-to-person team defence. Positional team defence where the team members defend within an area (or zone) is followed by dispossessing opponents.

Net game progressions begin with rallying co-operatively using depth and width, then introduce the use of short and long areas of the court. Drop, lob shots and volleys are used to encourage individual attacking and defensive strategies. Volleyball-type activity is introduced in year 5 and developed in year 6.

Fielding game progressions embody the principle of maximum participation with choice for the batter.

Sector games are employed to develop the batter's attacking skills and understanding. Co-operation between batter and bowler is introduced before competition. Batter and bowler versus two fielders precedes three versus one, four versus four and five versus five fielding games.

The principles of hitting for distance with a small bat are introduced alongside the use of a cricket-bat shape. Progression is used as a teaching strategy in a spiral structure. The material is designed for a specific age of pupil but its difficulty depends upon pupils' previous experience. Teachers may find that some classes need to revise strategies and skills from previous year group material.

H   Planning for the National Curriculum
The planning process

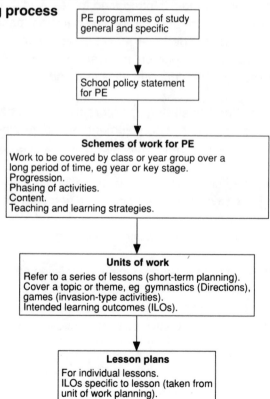

PE programmes of study
general and specific

School policy statement
for PE

Schemes of work for PE
Work to be covered by class or year group over a
long period of time, eg year or key stage.
Progression.
Phasing of activities.
Content.
Teaching and learning strategies.

Units of work
Refer to a series of lessons (short-term planning).
Cover a topic or theme, eg gymnastics (Directions),
games (invasion-type activities).
Intended learning outcomes (ILOs).

Lesson plans
For individual lessons.
ILOs specific to lesson (taken from
unit of work planning).

Planning decisions

Each school will have to decide how it is going to cover the PE National Curriculum. Factors concerning the games curriculum might include phasing (the time of year when activities are to be taught); the amount of time devoted to games and athletics and how that time is distributed (eg summer term – a block of time when all PE lessons are devoted to athletics and games – or weekly diet).

From these decisions a whole school policy can be produced which will form the basis of a delivery plan for key stage 2 games.

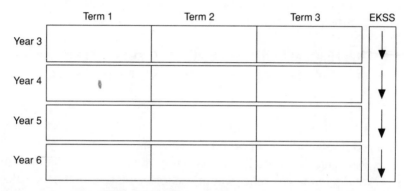

	Term 1	Term 2	Term 3	EKSS
Year 3				
Year 4				
Year 5				
Year 6				

Planning decisions for class teachers

● Unit of work: consider previous units of work and identify areas that need development/revisiting; consider the intended learning outcomes (ILOs) for the unit and break them down into a progressive series of lesson ILOs.

● Check the logical nature of lesson planning: decide which teaching strategies should be most appropriate; list resources (child/teacher) to be used; identify the criteria on which to make comments about pupils; prepare an assessment grid or criterion wheel.

● Write lesson plans which contain detailed ILOs, tasks and teaching points and the appropriate lesson structure

I **Assessment**

Assessment in physical education is carried out by observing children in practical, physical activities. Its purpose is to:
● identify children's achievements
● diagnose learning difficulties
● measure progress through the National Curriculum programmes of study.

Such information about pupils' achievements can tell us if the ILOs are being achieved; help in planning activities resulting in modified ILOs; provide feedback to pupils, other teachers and parents; and provide a basis for curriculum evaluation: eg content, resources, planning and teaching strategies.

The National Curriculum Statutory Assessment Framework consists of end of key stage statements for key stage 1 (years 1 and 2 and key stage 2 (years 3, 4, 5 and 6).

Formative and summative assessments during the key stage will contribute to the report on pupils' achievements at the end of each key stage (ie ages 7 and 11). This implies that criteria for formative and summative assessment are formulated from the end of key stage statements.

Note: End of key stage statements are designed to describe what the majority of children can be expected to achieve at the ages of 7 and 11.

Planning and assessment

Formative assessments enable the teacher to identify the next stages in a child's learning. The three strands identified in the PE National Curriculum are planning, performing and evaluating.

Children will progress at different rates in relation to each of these categories (eg levels of physical maturity). To enable children to achieve at their own level, tasks can be set as follows:
● as a common task for all children allowing for differentiated outcomes from different children

● at different levels of difficulty in relation to each task for different children or groups of children.

Pupils should be encouraged to assess their own and others' achievements by using specific criteria.

Collecting evidence of achievements
The main means is by direct observation. A number of performances must be observed before stating that a child is capable of performing a specific task (valid evidence).

The teacher can collect evidence of childrens' planning and evaluation by observing their physical performance, eg:
● in a change of strategy in a partner game
● understanding the changing role of defence and attack
● hitting to an undefended sector.

Pupils can add to this evidence in oral or written form (eg, recording their own performances in athletics). Evidence of achievement will be observed in:
● physical skill
● selection and organisation of response to a task (eg, making up a game; organising rules)
● appreciation by the pupil of their own and other pupils' (and adults') performances.

During games some children will display considerable physical skill but limited understanding of, for example, strategies for attack or defence; others will be able to understand the strategies, but lack the physical skills to carry out the strategy effectively, therefore teacher assessment needs to be organised to allow all pupils the opportunity to reveal what they can do and what they know and understand.

Methods of recording
Take the ILOs for a unit of work from the year group planner at the beginning of each year group scheme, break them down into lesson plan ILOs and write these as 'can do' performance statements. Use a grid or criterion wheel format to record assessments.

Unit				Summative comment at end of unit
	Lesson 1	Lesson 2	Lesson 3	
Name of child	ILOs	ILOs	ILOs	

criterion wheel

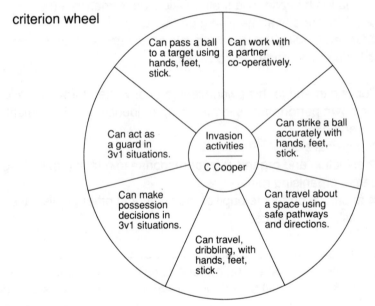

This 'evidence' can be coded

☐ Introduced by teacher

⊠ One piece of evidence

⊠ Evidence of mastery; several pieces of evidence

It is not necessary or possible to record in writing all the assessments you make. You will be able to observe only two or three children systematically during a games lesson, however, over the four years of key stage 2 you will be able to build up a very comprehensive picture of each child's games performance.

J Equipment

Large-/medium-sized plastic inflatable balls
● round 6.5" to 8.5" (max size 4)
● rugby-ball shape   .
● sponge/vinyl-coated sizes 3 and 4.

Small balls
● tennis ball cores
● sponge (vinyl coated) 7 cm and 9 cm
● glow/unburstable 7 cm (excellent for net/fielding activities)
● airflight/gamester-type 7 cm and 9 cm (for fielding and unihoc)
● shuttlecocks.

Bats
● wooden padder bats with short handles in a variety of shapes
● cricket-bat shapes of various sizes
● unihoc sticks
● rounders bats.

For marking out, targets, skills practices, etc
● plastic cones of various sizes
● bean bags
● quoits
● ropes of different lengths
● hoops of various sizes
● wire skittles (useful for making nets)
● garden canes 4' – 6' (useful for making 'nets')
● braids.

Storage of equipment
If equipment is bought in four different colours it can be stored in plastic crates/baskets with a variety of balls and bats. This enables the teacher to establish colour-coded apparatus areas and groups to

aid organisation and safety when getting out or putting away
apparatus.

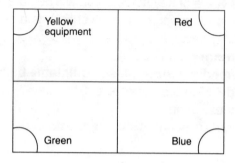

K   Space

Playgrounds can be organised into playing areas by marking grids
8 m x 8 m or 10 m x 10 m. Blocks of four are useful for developing
games. Grids are extremely useful for structuring groups of children;
they provide a flexible playing area for most games, and allow the
teacher maximum observation opportunity.

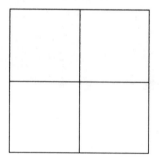
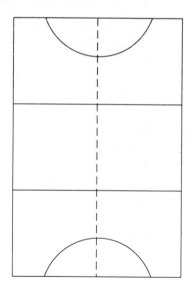

A netball court can be lined down the middle to provide six grids.
Grids can also be marked on grass.

Illustrations and diagrams

Numerous illustrations and diagrams are used to demonstrate the most significant features teachers should be looking for as the children carry out the practices and games.

Frequently occurring features have been given symbols which are used throughout the book:

●　　target – cone, skittle or bean bag

——　ropes or chalked lines, to mark boundaries or courts

6　　distance – the number and line indicate paces

○　　hoop – usually used as a 'target area' or base

★　　a task which can be used for athletics

PR　progression of a task.

These features will only be labelled if they are used in a way, or for a purpose, different from the one indicated in this key.

1 National Curriculum guidance – games

C5 Games
Key stage 1

4.13 At the beginning of KS1 pupils should be allowed to play freely. Lessons should be designed to give maximum activity as well as scope for individual exploration and practice. At this key stage lessons usually involve small apparatus such as airflow balls of assorted sizes, bean bags, hoops, quoits, skipping ropes, small, medium and larger sized balls and playbats of assorted shapes and sizes and, where appropriate, specially designed equipment for pupils with physical disabilities. The skills learned will help towards successful work with a partner and in small groups and are important for future success in games.

4.14 Units of work for approximately half a term could be developed to include aspects listed below.
● Footwork: running, hopping, skipping.
● Awareness of space and other people: chasing, dodging, avoiding.
● Jumping and landing.
● Ball skills: sending using hands and feet and incorporating hitting; receiving; travelling with a ball.
● Games: opportunity to make up and play games with simple rules and objectives that involve one person and with a partner when ready.

Key stage 2

4.15 During KS2 pupils should be given chances to increase their mastery of the skills of sending, receiving and travelling with a ball through practice, as well as learning new skills such as the overhead pass, catching a ball whilst running and dribbling a ball at speed around obstacles. As pupils proceed through KS2 their level of skill should increase and they will want to measure their own skills against opponents in small-sided games. Fair play is important and rules are necessary to regulate and improve play.

4.16 Possible units of work are listed below.
● Skills: further mastery of the skills identified in KS1, leading to work with or against another pupil and the development of an understanding of the principles of attack and defence.
● Small-sided games: the introduction to small-sided games created by the pupils or the teacher, including versions of invasion games like hockey, football, netball or rugby; playing games across nets or against walls; versions of striking or fielding games like cricket, rounders, softball or stoolball.

C3 Athletic activities
Key stage 1
4.5 A possible list of units of work taken from the PoS for KS1 is given below.
● Running: including speed work and non-competitive longer runs.
● Jumping: for accuracy, height and distance.
● Throwing: accurately, high, low and for distance.

Key stage 2
4.6 Possible units of work at KS2 are listed below.
● Running: sprinting up to 100 metres, relays (receiving and giving batons), shuttle relays.
● Running: training for non-competitive distance runs.
● Jumping: standing broad jumps, running long jumps, high jumps where facilities are appropriate.
● Throwing: rounders/cricket ball from a scratch line and with a run for accuracy and distance, soccer ball throw, simple shot putt.
● Competitions: those made up by the teacher and by the pupils.

4.7 In each unit there should be opportunities for pupils to measure and compare their own performances.

(Source – Non-Statutory Guidance PE National Curriculum).

Appendix

2   End of key stage statements and programmes of study (general) key stage 2

End of key stage statements
By the end of the key stage pupils should be able to:
● plan, practise, improve and remember more complex sequences of movement
● perform effectively in activities requiring quick decision-making
● respond safely, alone and with others, to challenging tasks, taking account of levels of skill and understanding.

Programme of study (general)
Pupils should:
● be assisted to plan, refine and adapt performance when working with others
● be encouraged to develop, consolidate and combine physical skills through practice and rehearsal
● be enabled to remember, select and repeat a range of movements and perform a range of more complex sequences alone and with others
● be encouraged to plan and use simple tactics and judge their success
● be enabled to respond quickly to changing environments or adjust to other people's actions
● be helped to explore and present different responses to a variety of tasks and stimuli
● be given opportunities to work alone to ensure the development of their own personal skills
● be encouraged to adopt good sporting behaviour and recognise and reject antisocial responses including unfair play.

3   Key stage 2 programme of study (activity specific)
Athletic activities
Pupils should:
● practise and develop basic actions in running (over short and longer distances and in relays), throwing and jumping
● be given opportunities for and guidance in measuring, comparing and improving their own performance, experience competitions, including those they make up themselves.

26

Appendix

Games

Pupils should individually, with a partner and in small groups:

● explore and be guided to an understanding of common skills and principles, including attack and defence, in invasion, net/wall and striking/field games

● be helped to improve the skills of sending, receiving and travelling with a ball for invasion, net/wall and striking/field games

● be given opportunities to develop their own games practices, working towards objectives decided sometimes by themselves and sometimes by the teacher, make up, play and refine their own games within prescribed limits, considering and developing rules and scoring systems.

(Source: Physical Education in the National Curriculum, DES)

| Invasion Unit | Intended learning outcomes: PoS to be covered |

Skills	Decisions/strategies
L1 Footwork: dodging, changes of direction, stopping. **Hands:** bouncing medium/large ball. **Rolling:** underarm aiming, downward cradle.	Attack/defend targets using rolling. Choosing undefended target (attacking decision). Anticipating the direction of attack (defensive decision). Deciding rule structure.
L2 Footwork: jogging, jumping and landing. **Hands:** bouncing and moving (medium/large ball) bounce pass, upward cradle.	Attack/defend targets using bouncing decisions as L1.
L3 Footwork: speeding up; slowing down. **Feet:** dribbling/control left and right feet; inside foot pass left and right feet.	Attack/defend targets using passing decisions as L1.
L4 Feet: dribbling the ball using inside and outside of feet; stopping using top of feet; dribbling around obstacles; 'wedge' trap.	Passing and trapping decisions as L1.
L5: Dribbling the ball (**unihoc stick**) around obstacles; passing through targets; dribble and pass.	Passing and trapping; moving into line to receive.
L6: Control around obstacles using hands or feet or unihoc stick. Development of control with other people and obstacles in the space. Moving and passing with a partner.	Looking up to see where obstacles are, at the same time monitoring position of the ball. Moving into space with a partner (without opposition); going forwards.

28

Net Unit — Intended learning outcomes: PoS to be covered

Skills	Decisions/strategies
L1 Footwork: following a partner (pathway and direction). **Small ball:** bouncing; rolling underarm to downward cradle; with several bounces; with one bounce rolling through a target/s.	**Aiming game:** rolling. **Attack:** use of width; use of feint or dummy; choosing undefended target. **Defence:** regaining the centre to reduce the angle for attacker; moving into line behind the ball. Appreciation of changing role between in possession (attack) and receiver (defence) in net game.
L2 Batting in the air; underarm 'feed' to hit; backhand and forehand hitting.	Hitting after top of the bounce. **Rally:** co-operative net game. Develop concept of depth.

Fielding Unit — Intended learning outcomes: PoS to be covered

Skills	Decisions/strategies
L1 Bouncing a small ball left and right hand. Bounce and catch: downward cradle. Overarm throw to downward cradle.	Bounce and catch game. Receiver: anticipation of direction of ball.
L2 Bouncing a small ball on the move; downward cradle catching.	Throwing for accuracy and distance to targets of different sizes and distances.
L3 Hitting with a padder bat. Bouncing with a bat. Hitting for distance and accuracy to a target (stance/arm action).	Timing of hitting for success. Hitting into a sector for accuracy. Understanding of stance/footwork in order to hit into different sector spaces.

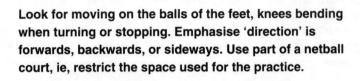

* **A.** Jog, changing direction each time I say 'change'. Use curving pathways, weaving in and out.

Look for moving on the balls of the feet, knees bending when turning or stopping. Emphasise 'direction' is forwards, backwards, or sideways. Use part of a netball court, ie, restrict the space used for the practice.

B. (i) Take a medium or large ball. Count how many bounces you can make without stopping.

For control insist on finger ends and thumb to bounce the ball, not the palm. The hand follows the ball during the bounce; the forearm moves, the elbow is a fixed pivot.

PR – Use dominant hand or a smaller ball.

B. (ii) With a partner. Stand ten paces apart. Roll the ball to each other, through the cones.

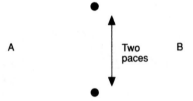

A   Two   B
               paces

The sender has one hand underneath the ball, which should be swung backwards then forwards. Stance sideways. The receiver must watch the sender's hands and the whole flight of the ball.

This practice teaches the receivers to watch the senders' actions so they can decide where the ball will arrive.

PR – Ask children if they can make the task more difficult, eg introduce more targets.

Equipment

A variety of plastic inflatable balls, ropes, four targets (skittles, cones, hoops or bean bags).

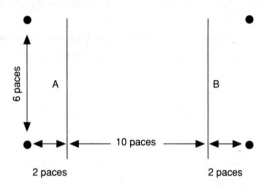

Target

A rolls the ball from behind the rope to try to hit B's targets (attack). B tries to intercept before the ball hits the target (defence), but must stand behind the rope line. B now has possession and the game proceeds.

Look for

Sender: accurate rolling, if not look at backswing and position of feet. Receiver: anticipating where the ball will arrive; if failing, direct their attention to sender's action. Both players should be moving on the balls of their feet, and choosing the undefended target to attack.

Ask

Where are you going to stand to receive the ball? If you stop a scoring pass, which target will you aim at next? Are there any rules both players must follow?

Develop

What happens when the targets are moved wider/ closer? Are they easier to defend or attack? Invent a game using three/four targets.

* A. Jog, dodging and weaving. Remember to use different directions to avoid collisions. On the signal, jump high into the air from a one-foot take-off, land in balance, and continue moving on curved pathways.

The children should remain inside the area set for this safety practice for all landings. Landings which are balanced should be on the balls of the feet, knees bending, arms spread wide, body held upright. A rebound should follow each 'give' landing, before the children continue moving.

B. (i) Take a medium or large ball. Can you keep the ball bouncing as you move?

The ball is bounced to the side of the body, not in front, to avoid it being bounced on to the foot as they move. Ask the children to move forwards, backwards and sideways, and to count the number of bounces. Begin walking, progress to jogging.

B. (ii) With a partner. Stand five paces apart. Pass the ball to each other so that it bounces once.

Safety: Receiver: arms out, upward cradle, cushion the ball by bending elbows as the ball arrives.

Some children will toss the ball upwards to achieve a bounce. Ask them if they can find a way of holding the ball so that they can push it downwards as they bounce pass. The receiver, hands ready to catch or stop the ball, must watch the whole flight from their partner's hands.

PR – Ask the children to invent a passing/bouncing game using three hoops.

Equipment
As for **Target Roll** (see Invasion Unit Lesson 1).

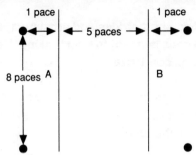

Target
The sender has to use a bounce pass, ie the ball bouncing at least once on its way to the target. The receiver tries to catch the ball after one bounce to prevent it hitting the target.

Look for
Downward bouncing of the ball. Receiver watching the sender's actions closely. The children developing strategies to achieve a hit (attack) or an interception (defence).

Ask
What attack strategies are you using (eg dummy or feint pass to deceive the defender)? How will you intercept? Anticipate the direction of the pass and get into line behind the ball.

Develop
If more than two targets are used this will lead to more careful concentration by the receiver on the sender's action. The sender will have to decide which is the best target to aim at (attack) by considering the defender's position. Change partners several times.

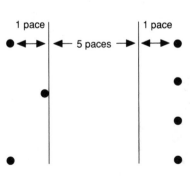

A. Jog lightly on the balls of your feet. On signal, speed up and then slow down gradually. Repeat.

Look for quick, short strides and arms pumping to accelerate, knees bending to help braking. Use a large area, eg netball court size.

B. (i) Take a large ball. Using the inside and outside of your feet can you dribble the ball keeping it close to your feet all the time?

Use a large space to minimise collisions. Begin at walking pace. Emphasise the use of both feet, and which parts of the foot are used to turn the ball to the left and right.

B. (ii) With a partner. Stand ten paces apart and pass the ball to each other using the inside of your foot. Receiver stops the ball before returning it.

The sender must watch the ball as it is kicked. The non-kicking foot should be placed alongside the ball and should point to the receiver. The kicking foot strikes the ball at a right angle to the non-kicking foot, thus ensuring that the pass travels straight to the target. Passes will go astray at first; ask what happens to the pass if the inside of the foot is not facing the target.

PR – Try sidefoot passing using left foot and right foot.

Equipment

A large ball, two/four ropes or chalked lines, two targets.

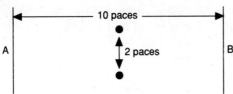

Target

A passes the ball from the line through the targets to B. B traps the ball near their own line and returns the ball through the targets.

Look for

Points in B(ii): if aim is poor increase the space between the targets, and at the same time draw the passer's attention to foot positioning as the ball is struck. Is the non-kicking foot facing towards the target?

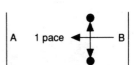

Ask

How can you make this more challenging (eg narrow the space between targets)?

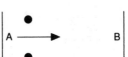

Develop

Vary the position and spacing of the targets. Increase the length of the pass.

Use two offset targets, and ask the children to decide the rules for this variation.

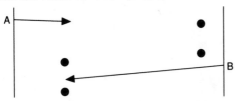

35

A. Take any ball. Using the inside and outside of your feet, can you move keeping the ball under control?

Begin at walking pace. Encourage the children to try different types and sizes of ball. Restrict the area used (two-thirds of a netball court).

B. (i) Dribble a large ball anywhere inside the area. On the signal, stop the ball using the bottom of your foot. When the ball is still, continue dribbling once more.

Use the bottom of the foot to trap the ball. Practice stopping the ball with the left and the right foot. Practice pushing the ball forwards (sideways, backwards), with the bottom of the foot to begin dribbling again.

PR – Introduce a number of cones, bean bags, quoits, etc into the space. Repeat task. This makes children use their peripheral vision to watch for obstacles as well as keeping control.

B. (ii) With a partner. Stand ten paces apart. Mark the passing area with skipping ropes. Pass the ball to each other using the inside of the foot. Stop the ball behind the rope with the bottom of your foot before returning it to your partner.

Wedge trap will be most successful. Look for the receiver getting into a position to trap the ball by moving into line behind the direction of the pass using skilful footwork. Draw the receiver's attention to the sender's foot in order to make a prediction about where the ball will arrive.

PR – Ask the children to use three cones, etc to invent a pass/trap game.

Target Trap
A trapping game for two players.

Equipment
A large ball, four ropes or chalked lines.

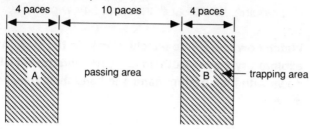

Target
A passes from within the trapping area, marked by the ropes. B traps the ball within the trapping area before returning the ball to A.

Look for
Accurate passing using the sides of the foot. Getting quickly into line behind the pass in order to make a successful wedge trap. Moving on the balls of the feet.

Ask
What rules can you invent for this game?

Develop
What happens if you decrease the width of the trapping area? Difficulty of the game is increased as trapping has to be more skilful.

How can you make the game more challenging? Increase length of passing area so that angled passes require the receiver to move quickly into line.

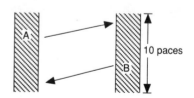

How would this change your tactics, or the scoring? Use of left and right foot to trap the ball.

Where would you place targets to make the game harder? How would they affect the rules and scoring?

A. Take a unihoc stick and a small ball. Move about keeping the ball close to the stick. Avoid collisions by stopping the ball and choosing a new pathway.

Watch how and where the children hold the stick. At this exploratory stage ask them to try holding the stick lower down with their bottom hand and bend their knees on the move.

B. (i) Introduce obstacles into the space (as A Lesson 6).

B. (ii) With a partner. Stand ten paces apart. Place two targets halfway between you and hit the ball through the targets to each other.

Grip for right-hander: hold the stick on the right-hand side of the body, the right hand further down the stick than the left hand. The right palm should face away from the body, the left palm towards the body. Reverse this grip for left-handers. Place hands fairly close together for passing. Swing the stick backwards and then forwards to hit the ball. Try to keep the head of the stick below waist height.

Equipment
Unihoc sticks, cones, etc, a variety of small balls.

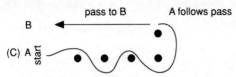

Target
A dribbles ball around the cones and passes back to B. B traps the ball and repeats the practice.

Look for
Careful push-pass keeping head of the stick close to the floor; ball under control – keep the speed down. Both sides of the stick can be used – this is not hockey!

Ask
How can you make this game more difficult?
● make obstacle angles greater

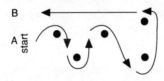

● introduce more obstacles

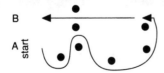

● reduce spaces between obstacles
● have a target to pass through to get the ball to B.

Develop
Smooth control and timing of pass. Experiment with a variety of small balls. Keep groups small to increase participation.

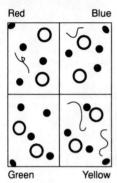

Red   Blue

Green   Yellow

A. Scatter obstacles in the grids (bean bags, hoops, ropes, cones). Take any ball. Using any part of your feet, move around the obstacles keeping the ball under control.

Let children experiment with the challenge of a variety of balls. Look for control with both feet, stopping ball before a collision with obstacle or other people, and using the appropriate part of foot to turn round an obstacle.

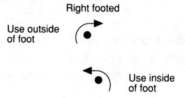

Right footed

Use outside of foot

Use inside of foot

PR – Use hands. Use unihoc sticks.

B. (i) Mix the colours of equipment in the four grids. Give each child a colour. Go on a journey visiting all the obstacles of your own colour.

Encourage stopping and looking up for next colour obstacle. Begin walking, progress to jogging. This introduces the child to looking for a defender or a person on their own side while controlling/ keeping possession of the ball.

PR – Use hands. Use unihoc sticks.

B. (ii) With a partner. One ball between two, travel in the space passing the ball to each other.

Ask the children how they can move and pass at the same time.

Moving and Passing — A game for two players.

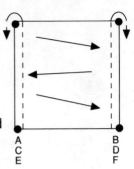

Equipment
A variety of balls, unihoc sticks, one grid space and four cones per group.

Target
A moves forwards then passes to B, who moves forwards and passes to A, etc. At the end of the grid they jog back to the start. As soon as A and B are halfway, C and D start, etc.

```
A      B
C      D
E      F
```

Encourage moving forwards and passing sideways. Start with passing with hands – a swing pass is usually easiest. Progress to unihoc, then feet.

Ask
Where will you need to send the ball so that your partner can catch, pass, hit it without stopping? Answer: slightly in front!

Develop
Use a variety of equipment.

Look for
Speed of passing.
Correct foot when using feet.

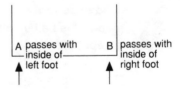

A passes with inside of left foot   B passes with inside of right foot

This practice develops moving forward into space without opposition.

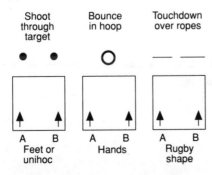

Shoot through target	Bounce in hoop	Touchdown over ropes
A B	A B	A B
Feet or unihoc	Hands	Rugby shape

A. With a partner. Partner A leads, jogging, partner B follows, trying to keep as close to partner A as possible. When the signal to stop is given, partner B should be within touching distance of A. Partner B becomes leader. Repeat.

Use the netball court. Emphasise the footwork skills learned in Invasion Unit Lessons 3 and 4, especially changes in direction and speed for the leader, and stopping safely for the follower.

B. (i) Take a small ball. Count how many bounces you can make without stopping. Can you do five bounces, ten bounces, etc?

NB Use a ball which bounces the same every time like a tennis ball or the core of a tennis ball. Any ball which has a seam, like a sponge bouncer, will not make the same response each time and this is confusing and frustrating for your pupils.

Eyes should be kept on the ball. The tips of the fingers are used to control the force and direction of push. The hand follows the ball up and down as it bounces, but the elbow is kept still.

B. (ii) With a partner. Stand ten paces apart and roll the ball to each other. The receiver watches the sender's action from backswing to receiving the ball using a downward cradle. Make sure the receiver shows the cradle before the ball is sent. This is a very important safety point for later catching practices.

PR – Send the ball with several bounces. Send the ball with one bounce.

A rolling and receiving game for two players.

Equipment

A small ball, two ropes or chalked lines, two bean bags, two padder bats.

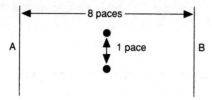

Target

A rolls the ball with a bat, from the line through the bean bags to B, who must stand behind the rope to receive it. B traps the ball then returns the ball to A.

Look for

Sender: a smooth hit with no bounces – look at backswing, knees bending, sideways stance.
Receiver: getting quickly into line behind the path of the ball, solving how to stop/trap the ball.

Ask

How can you make this game harder? Make the space between the bean bags smaller (is this harder for the sender or receiver?); make the distance longer.

Develop

How could you use two more bean bags to make the game more difficult? How would this change your tactics?

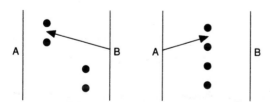

Attack: dummy or feint, or use width of pass to draw defender out of position. Defence: try to regain the centre position after each pass to reduce the angle and space given to the attacker.

A. Take a small bat and ball. How many times can you bounce the ball on the bat?

Use a sponge, gamester or glow ball. Keep the bat face level, wrist firm. Bend at the shoulder rather than the elbow for upward movement. Hit gently.

B. (i) Take a small bat and a ball. Can you make small bounces in the air? Make larger bounces in the air?

B. (ii) Can you let the ball bounce once on the ground then keep it in the air for two hits?

The angle of the bat controls the direction of the hit. If the children angle the bat's face towards them, the ball disappears over their shoulder. They should watch the ball hit the bat, and keep a stiff wrist as they hit.

If some children are not succeeding try one bounce on the floor followed by one hit in the air. Progress to one bounce on the floor, two in the air, etc. Let them experiment with different bat shapes, and small balls, in order to find successful combinations.

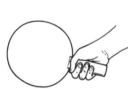

B. (iii) With a partner. One hoop, a small ball (9 cm vinyl foam or glow), one bat. A throws the ball gently underarm or overarm into the hoop. B hits the ball back to A. Change after five hits. Repeat.

The hoop allows the hitter to know the direction and trajectory of the ball. Look for sideways stance and hitting the ball after the top of the bounce, upwards, back to the receiver. Grip the bat as far up the handle as possible.

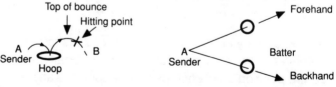

PR – Use two hoops. Introduce forehand and backhand.

44

Equipment

Small ball, two bats, four ropes.

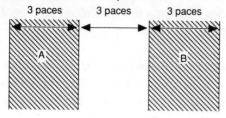

Target

A and B rally, trying to bounce the ball in the hatched areas. This is a co-operative game designed to practice net-type hitting skills, and teach the principle of hitting deep or long. Start with a bounce serve.

Look for

Correct timing of hit (see B(iii)) and sideways stance. Allow children to control the ball any number of times before returning it.

Ask

Where do you need to hit the ball so that your partner can return it easily? What trajectory do you need to use to keep the rally going? What happens when you alter the sizes of the areas?

Develop

Making correct early decision where the ball will arrive by the receiver watching the sender's hand action. Introduce bean bag/quoit sidelines. Ask the children to invent the rules for a co-operative game, using the width and depth of the court.

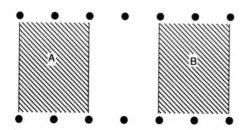

A. Take a small ball. Bounce the ball. Can you use your right and left hand? Make small, fast bounces; large, slow ones? Bounce the ball from left to right and back again?

Look for skills mentioned in Net Unit, especially the smooth movement of the hand following the ball. Ask which type of bounce best keeps the ball under control.

B. (i) Take a small ball. Throw the ball up into the air, let it bounce, then catch it in two hands.

A downward catching cradle should be used. As the ball touches the hands, the fingers are curled around the ball, the elbows bend and the hands are brought towards the chest. The children should watch the ball closely. Ask 'Can you let the ball bounce twice (three times), before you catch it?'

B. (ii) With a partner. Stand five paces apart. Can you bounce the ball to your partner to make it reach them at waist height?

Sender: holds the ball between thumb and first and second fingers, bouncing the ball with a downward action. Receiver: shows downward catching cradle, stops or catches the ball, then returns it with a bounce which will make the ball reach their partner at waist height. Ask 'Where will you have to bounce the ball to make it arrive at waist height?'

Hoop Bounce

A bouncing and catching game for two players.

Equipment

Small ball, two ropes or chalked lines, one hoop.

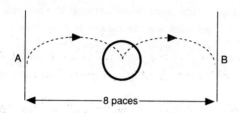

Target

A stands behind the line and sends the ball to B making it bounce in the hoop. B returns the ball in the same way.

Look for

Sender: downward bouncing into hoop; overarm throw. Receiver: watching the whole flight of the ball, using a downward cradle and good footwork to get into line behind the path of the ball.

Ask

Can you invent a scoring system? Will a catch or an accurate bounce score?

Develop

Increase the size of the pitch. Use a smaller hoop. Use two hoops. Ask the children to set their own positions, eg:

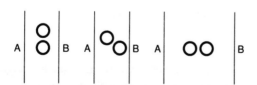

The receiver must watch the sender's action very carefully in order to predict into which target the ball will be thrown.

A. Take a small ball. Can you move about, bouncing the ball and keeping it under control?

Restrict the practice area: work around the outside noticing children who are losing control. Remind them of the skills learned in Net Unit. Suggest they begin moving at walking pace (more confident children will be able to move more quickly). Ask the children to use both hands as they move and good footwork to weave in and out.

B. (i) Using a medium ball, bean bag, then a small ball, can you throw it into the air and catch it (five times, ten times, etc), without letting it bounce?

Children should use a downward catching cradle. After the ball has been thrown upwards with an underarm action, the arms stretch out, fingers pointing at the ball. The fingers curl around the ball when it touches them, the elbows bend and the hands are brought close to the chest. As the ball is caught the knees should bend to cushion the catch.

Do not worry about children who get their hands in the right place but drop the ball; they have made an accurate prediction about where the ball will arrive. Look for those who miss the ball. Are they watching the whole flight? Are their fingers pointing at the ball as it descends towards them?

B. (ii) With a partner. Stand five paces apart. Throw the ball to your partner. Count how many catches you can make together before I call 'stop'.

Use skill techniques introduced in B(i). Sender: uses backswing learned in rolling the ball to toss the ball underarm. Receiver: watches the whole flight of the ball, makes a downward cradle target.
NB Accuracy in throwing is important if the catching part of the practice is to be successful.

A game for groups of six players.

Equipment

Ropes or chalked lines, hoops (different sizes), targets (skittles or cones); quoits, bean bags (three each).

```
1
2   Quoits
3
```

```
4   Bean
5   bags
6
```

Target

Players throw from behind the line aiming at different targets to encourage accuracy of throwing underarm. They score one point for each successful hit.

Safety: All throw, then all collect.

Look for

Smooth backswing and follow-through action. Ask: 'If you want the ball to go higher and further where do you release it, lower or higher?'. Bring their attention to the feeling of the throw, 'Do you need to throw harder or softer next time?'.

Ask

About the shape of the flight (trajectory) of the bean bag (quoit). Was it it too high or too low? Will each target score the same?

Develop

The distance and size of the targets.

Remind about safety procedure (same for athletics throws).

If you don't have enough equipment to do this as a class activity, have half the class working on **Hoop Bounce.**

A. Experiment with bouncing and catching, catching in the air and rolling and retrieving. Use a variety of apparatus, from balls to quoits and bean bags.

Emphasise the use of downward cradle and encourage children to evaluate their skill and how the equipment behaves, by questioning.

B. (i) Using a small bat, can you keep the ball bouncing against the ground? Count how many bounces you make.

Use bats which have a short handle. Let children experiment with oblong and round bats. To keep the ball bouncing the bat face must be level with the ground; any variation will send the ball off course. The wrist should be firm; the bat should be used as an extension of bouncing with the fingers.

PR – Can you do the same thing moving around the playground? Count how many bounces you make.

B. (ii) With a partner. A small ball, one bat, two hoops, two cones. A bowls under/overarm into the hoop, B hits the ball into the hoop behind A, who retrieves. Bowler and batter swop after five turns.

Hoop

Batter: sideways stance – begin hitting action as ball leaves the sender's hand.

PR – Through-the-air bowling. Increasing length of the hit.

50

Sector Hitting
A game for three players.

Equipment
A small ball, padder bat, two hoops, two cones.

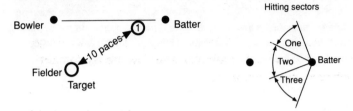

Bowler ● —————— ① ● Batter

10 paces

Fielder ○
Target

Hitting sectors

One
Two ● Batter
Three

Target
A bowls ball into hoop 1. Batter hits ball to target hoop. Fielder retrieves. Change roles after five hits.

Batter and bowler co-operate so that batter can practice hitting to sector three. Batter alters sideways stance by moving foot towards hoop 1 as ball is bowled, to turn body in direction of hit. Progress to through-the-air bowling. Fielder returns ball to bowler.

Develop
Place target hoop in sector one. How does this affect the position of the bowler's hoop and the position of the front foot of the batter?

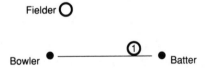

Fielder ○

Bowler ● —————— ① ● Batter

Progress to hitting game for four players (Fielding Unit Year 4 Lesson 2) which uses all three sectors.

| Invasion Unit | Intended learning outcomes: PoS to be covered |

Skills	Decisions/strategies
L1 Footwork: pathways and direction. **Hands:** bouncing medium/large ball; moving with obstacles. Bounce pass with signalling; upward cradle.	**Change Ball:** accurate passing. Looking up to locate the target; recognising the signal; scanning. Using a signal to ask for the ball. Develop using feet/unihoc.
L2 Footwork: carrying a ball in two hands. Travelling and bouncing using **hands**. Chest pass, upward cradle. Partners: passing on the move.	**Possession (3 v 1)** introduction of opposition: uneven sides (three attack) develops principle of how to keep possession (attack); who to pass to, when and where to pass; moving into a free space to receive; signalling for the ball; understanding of attack triangle. Defensive strategies not introduced but questions asked – will guard mark a person or the spaces between persons? Children decide rule structure.
L3: Bouncing and carrying the ball. **Change Ball** (hands, feet, unihoc). **Possession** (hands, feet, unihoc). Passing, signalling, catching, dribbling, with and without opposition. Uneven sides to favour attack. Rule structure decided by children.	Emphasis on common principles using hands, feet and stick. **Attack (3 v 1)** introduces moving forwards to score with opposition. Decisions as possession for **Attack** and defence. Introduces attacking positions – wide left, centre, wide right.
L4: Putting down and picking up and carrying the ball. Swing passing to downward cradle (rugby-ball shape). Passing and moving forwards into space: partners, no opposition.	**Touch Down (3 v 3):** even-sided passing game to practice the principles of **Attack** **3 v 1** (scoring over/on end line).
L5: Dribbling with feet, with obstacles. Front foot pass. Revision of **Possession** and **Attack** before:	**Hit the Targets (3 v 3):** scoring through two goals. Decisions as **Possession**.
L6: Dribbling and control. Passing in confined space. Heading to a partner. Heading in different directions.	**Head Ball (3 v 3)**: scoring over an end line with the head. Decisions as **Possession**.

52

Invasion Unit cont   Intended learning outcomes: PoS to be covered

Skills	Decisions/strategies
L7: Unihoc dribbling with obstacles in space. Partner, travelling and passing forwards. Revise **Change Ball, Possession, Attack** with unihoc sticks.	**Hit the Targets** as L5. Narrow playing area makes defence easier; wider playing area makes attack easier. Concept of width in attack.

Net Unit   Intended learning outcomes: PoS to be covered

Skills	Decisions/strategies
L1: Padder bat control with upward and downward bounces. Rallying over a net space co-operatively. Revision of when to hit the ball. Use of hoops to practice particular types of shot.	**Hoops**: a rallying game which allows children to move hoops to adjust the game for themselves. Principles of attack – depth and width.
L2: Rallying with controlling hits. Problem-solve a net game: through-the-air rallies.	**Net Rally:** introduction of four-section long and short area court with net. Moving to anticipate shots which use depth (short shot) to attack. Development of rules using sidelines.

Fielding Unit   Intended learning outcomes: PoS to be covered

Skills	Decisions/strategies
L1: Travelling, throwing and catching a small ball. Underarm throw, downward cradle. Overarm throw, upward cradle.	**Pressure Throw** develops accurate judgment of force and trajectory of throwing action.
L2: Underarm and overarm throwing for accuracy. Partner hitting – backswing, stance, with a bounce, through the air.	**Non-stop Hitting**: Batter v bowler and two fielders. Batter: how, when and where to hit. Fielders: where the ball will arrive and how to send it to the bowler.
L3: Problem-solving a target throwing game. Cricket-bat shape/padder bat hitting to sectors. Movement of feet/stance in order to hit to a designated space. Fielding skills: stopping, catching, throwing.	Bowler and batter co-operate in order to hit the ball to the fielder. Introduction of hitting sectors. **Non-stop Hitting**: bowler and batter co-operate against two fielders. Cricket-bat shape; circular-type playing area. **Bowler**: where to pitch the ball to help batter hit into undefended space. **Batter**: to look for undefended space. **Fielders**: as L2.

53

A. Jog on curving pathways and on the signal, stop.

★ Use part of a netball court or a restricted space. Look for moving lightly on the balls of the feet, knees bending to dodge and to stop, arms helping with balance. There should be no collisions as the children move forwards, sideways and backwards around each other.

PR – Partners: A leading, B following. Change on signal.

B. (i) Take a large ball and begin bouncing in a space of your own. Count the number of bounces you make.

Look for use of left and right hand; the fingers, not palm, controlling the ball; the elbow 'fixed', the forearm moving with the bounce.

PR – Moving and bouncing. Introduce obstacles in space (Invasion Unit Lesson 6 Year 3).

B. (ii) With a partner. Stand five paces apart. Bounce the ball to each other so that it arrives at waist height.

Receiver makes an upward catching cradle – arms outstretched ready to bring hands into chest and elbows out – as the ball is received. Concentrate on the receiver at this stage; allow the sender to work out the best way to achieve the task.

PR – Practice sending so that you move your partner to the side (left and right). Partner signals with hands where they want the ball sent. Travel around passing the ball to each other using bounce passes.

Equipment

One grid space, a ball for the players inside the grid.

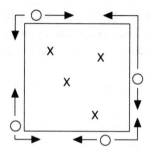

Target

Partner organisation. Players inside the grid travel about bouncing the ball. Players outside the grid jog around the outside ready to receive the ball on the signal of 'change' – partners then change roles.

Look for

Sender stopping and looking up to find partner (accurate passing). Receiver signalling for the ball by showing an upward cradle.This game teaches the player in possession to scan for their team mate, while controlling the ball.

Ask

Ask each partner group to invent a signalling system which is silent but allows them to know when to change.

Develop

Use chest and bounce passes. Use unihoc sticks (invent signalling). Use feet (invent signalling).

A. Travel around carrying a medium or large ball in both hands. Use curving pathways. On signal, throw the ball into the air and catch it as you jog.

Some children will need to walk to begin with. They must watch other people and monitor the ball and move – a lot of information to process!

B. (i) Move around bouncing a large ball.

Look for the use of left and right hands; bouncing the ball at the side of the body; avoiding collisions by stopping or dodging; small bounces for controlled turning and larger ones for moving on curving pathways.

PR – Introduce obstacles into the space.

B. (ii) With a partner. Stand five paces apart. Pass the ball to each other to reach your partner's chest.

Sender holds the ball in an upward cradle position and then pushes the ball forwards and slightly upwards. The arms are now outstretched; this is the receiver's upward cradle. As the ball is caught the receiver's arms bend at the elbows to absorb the energy of the pass. The elbows are kept out from the body when passing and receiving, the feet are placed backwards and forwards, knees flexed for moving into line quickly .

B. (iii) Travel around passing the ball to each other using a chest pass.

Look for accuracy of sending, good footwork, and signalling.

Equipment

One grid 10 m x 10 m (marked by ropes, bean bags, etc), a large ball (size 4 or smaller).

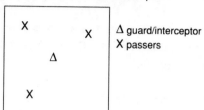

Δ guard/interceptor
X passers

Target

The passers have to make six passes without the guard touching the ball. If the guard touches the ball the player who made the intercepted pass becomes guard. If six passes are achieved, the player making the final pass becomes the guard.

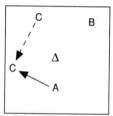

A has ball,
C and B are guarded.
C moves to free space
to receive pass from A.

Look for

Moving to a new space after passing the ball (a new space is one where a player is in a position to receive the ball); making the correct decision to pass to an unguarded player; moving on the balls of the feet; hands ready in an upward catching cradle; signalling.

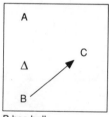

B has ball,
A is guarded.
B passes to C.

Ask

What sort of 'shape' in relation to each other is best for keeping possession? Answer: attack triangle. Why? Answer: there is always a free person to pass to.

Develop

How can the guard intercept (defensive strategies)? (If all overhead passes are used, negotiate a fairer deal: chest or bounce passes only!)

Will guard mark one person very closely or mark the space between two receivers?

Select groups to demonstrate effective strategies of possession (attack) and marking (defence).

A. With a partner. A with a ball. A leads, bouncing or carrying the ball, B follows. On signal, A stops, passes the ball to B who then leads.

Look for good co-operation and a range of appropriate passes: bounce, chest, swing. Encourage B to be moving as the pass is received.

B. (i) Revise **Change Ball**, some groups using unihoc sticks, some using feet, some hands. Rotate groups to vary equipment and skills used.

Emphasise the common invasion skills and strategies. (see Lesson 1).

B. (ii) Revise **Possession** using unihoc sticks, feet and hands.

This system of organisation allows a variety of skills to be used and maximises the use of equipment.

Equipment

One grid (10 m x 10 m), a medium/large ball, coloured braid for the defender, four marker cones.

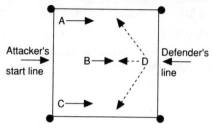

Target

A, B and C are attackers. Any one starts with the ball near the attackers' line. By passing the ball to each other they have to touch the ball down on the defender's line. D, the defender, tries to intercept, defending the line. The scoring player becomes D. If the defender is successful, the change is with the player who sent the intercepted pass and the game restarts at the attackers' line. This is a progression from **Possession**. Now the attackers are moving forward into space and need to keep the attack triangle intact.

Refer to the teaching points in **Possession** and concentrate on the attack co-operative strategies.

Ask

How would you describe positions for attackers? How do you keep to your attack triangle?

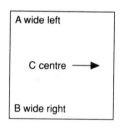

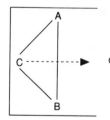 or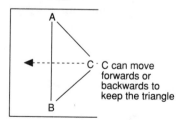

Develop

Similar invasion attack games using unihoc sticks, feet, and rugby-type ball. Develop strategies learned in even-sided games.

A. With a partner. One ball between two. One partner carries the ball, dodging and weaving, while the other partner follows. On signal, the carrier puts the ball down, the follower scoops up the ball and becomes the leader. Repeat.

Restrict the space used so that lots of dodging is necessary. Look for moving on the balls of the feet, scooping using two hands, and bending knees as the pick-up is made.

B. (i) With a partner. Stand five paces apart. Pass the ball so that it reaches your partner at waist height.

Ask, 'What is the best way to hold the ball?' Bring the arms to one side of the body. Swing the ball backwards then forwards, releasing the ball as your hands are pointing at your partner (right-handed players will find it easier to swing the ball to the right of their body with their left foot forward, vice-versa for left-handed players). Receiver makes a downward cradle, arms outstretched.

Try passing from the left and right side of the body.

B. (ii) With a partner. One grid (per four partner groups), one ball.

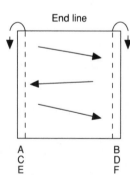

End line

Travel forwards passing the ball sideways. At the end of the grid jog back on the outside to the start.

Ask players where the pass needs to be sent to keep their partner on the move. Ask A to jog forward before passing. Keep close together to begin the practice.

A
C
E

B
D
F

PR – Touch down on end line.

B. (iii) Introduce the games of **Possession** and **Attack** before the following even-sided game.

Equipment

One 10 m x 10 m grid, a rugby/round-shaped ball, braids for one side.

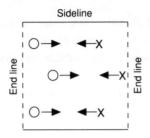

Target

To touch the ball down on the opposing team's end line.

Ask

How will you start the game? What happens after a score? How will you restart if the ball goes out of play at the sideline? What kind of passes will you use?

You may have to intervene to ensure that each player touches the ball, restrict the type of pass used and restrict running with the ball. Don't emphasise backward passes at this stage; passes can be in any direction.

Develop

In the excitement of the game the defenders usually have the upper hand. To increase attack opportunities play across two grids, widening the end line.

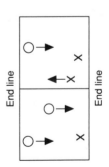

Defensive strategies are not introduced at this stage although person-to-person marking usually occurs. If appropriate, ask the children to decide rules about physical contact. (For defensive strategies see Invasion Unit Years 5 and 6.)

A. Take a large ball. Dribble the ball around, keeping control with the inside and outside of your feet. Keep inside the grid and on signal stop the ball.

Revision of Year 3 activity. Use a restricted space (two-thirds of a netball court). Emphasise that it is control of the ball rather than speed of the dribble you are looking for.

B. (i) Move around inside the grid and when you meet an obstacle use the outside of your foot to control the ball around it.

Place cones, skittles, small hoops or bean bags inside the grid at random. Children should begin at walking pace, keeping the ball close to the feet. Ask, 'If you approach an obstacle from the left which foot would you use to go round it (and vice-versa)?'.

B. (ii) With a partner. Stand ten paces apart. Pass to each other using the front of the foot. On receiving the ball either trap it before returning or pass it back without trapping.

In order to make a smooth rolling pass, the passing foot should be pointed, the eyes looking at the ball. Passing using the side of the foot should be revised before the following games.

B. (iii) Revise the games of **Possession** and **Attack** using feet.

Most children find foot skill control more difficult than using hands, therefore the defender should be restricted in challenging for the ball so that attacking strategies can be used successfully.

Refer to teaching points in Lessons 1, 2 and 3.

A passing game for six players (3 v 3).

Equipment

20 m x 10 m grid, a ball, four targets, cones, etc (placed in front of end lines), braids for one side.

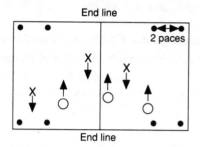

Target

To pass through either of opposing team's targets. Ask children to decide the rule structure of the game (see Invasion Unit Year 4 Lesson 4).

Look for

Side foot passing, front foot passing, and wedge trapping. Encourage calling for the ball but only when in a free space. Children will be preoccupied with control at first so do not expect a lot of passing until skills improve.

Ask

Two goals are provided. How does this help the attack? What happens if the goals are made smaller?

Develop

Try one large goal. How does this affect the scoring opportunities?

Emphasise the principles of possession, signalling, and attack triangle.

A. Move around inside the grid dribbling the ball. On the signal, stop your ball and exchange it with the person's nearest to you. Use a side or front foot pass. As soon as you receive a new ball, continue dribbling.

Look for accurate passing, and the speed of the pass. Ask the children to aim slightly to the side of the person they are passing to (let them decide which side). Encourage a pause between stopping the ball and passing, to look for someone to pass to.

B. (i) With a partner. Stand five paces apart. A holds the ball in front of the face then heads it towards B. B traps the ball before passing it back. After three heading turns, change over. Repeat.

The head and upper body are held back before the forehead moves forwards to strike the ball. Feet are placed backwards and forwards for good balance as the ball is struck. NB Use a light plastic or foam ball for this and other heading practices.

B. (ii) With a partner. Stand five paces apart. A serves the ball and B heads it back. After three serves change over. Repeat.

Look for feet backwards and forwards, knees flexed, with the weight on the back foot ready to move forwards to meet the ball. Receiver should watch the whole flight of the ball from the sender's hands, and try to keep their eyes open! The serve should be underarm and gentle.

B. (iii) Using a ball and two or three hoops of different sizes, invent a heading practice which develops B(ii).

Equipment
20 m x 10 m grid, a ball, four skittles, braids.

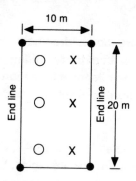

Target
To head the ball over the opposing team's end line.
The game is played with hands but to score, the
attack must use a header.

Safety: Use a large foam ball.

Ask
Children to decide the rule structure for this game.

Teamwork is important – emphasise getting into a free
space in order to try a scoring header.

Develop
Impose conditions on the game: for example, the
defenders must not handle the ball to prevent a score.
What other body parts could be used?

Goals to score into: design your own goals to suit this
game. How does the use of goals affect the attacking
and defensive strategies?

A. Take a unihoc stick and a small ball. Move about keeping the ball close to the stick. Can you stop the ball with the stick?

Watch how and where the children hold the stick. At this exploratory stage ask them to try holding the stick lower down, and to bend their knees a little more as they move about. Ask them to try this practice with different sorts of ball.

PR – Introduce obstacles (cones, ropes, beanbags, etc). Practice dribbling around the obstacles. Keep close control. Progress from walking to jogging.

B. (i) With a partner. Travel around the space passing the ball to each other.

Emphasise close control, trapping, and looking up before using a short push-pass.

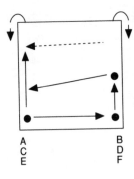

A
C
E

B
D
F

B. (ii) With a partner. Using a grid, passing and moving for the return. When passing, keep the pass a little in front of your partner.

This is a challenging skill and needs lots of practice; repetition in subsequent lessons.

B. (iii) Progress to **Change Ball**, **Possession** and **Attack** games before even-sided 3 v 3. **Hit the Targets** (Lesson 5) is a suitable unihoc game.

Invasion organisation

Invasion games can be played with feet, implements and hands using a variety of targets: eg scoring into a target; scoring through a target; scoring behind or on a line.

Bounce Ball Four large hoops, large ball, braids for one team	Score Eight cones, small ball, unihoc sticks, braids	Touch Down Four cones, rugby-ball shape, braids
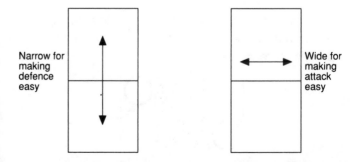		
Target: to bounce the ball in either of opponent's hoops. Safety: keep hoops inside grid and away from walls or curbs/ edges of playground.	Target: to score through opponent's cones. NB this game can be played with feet.	Target: to touch ball down on or behind opponent's line. Safety: make sure there is space behind line.

Begin with hands and progress to implements and feet. Game cards are useful to speed up organisation (safety, space, equipment, etc). Children can be asked to decide scoring and rule structure which releases the teacher to intervene in learning rather than in rule disputes!

Grids are essential for invasion games teaching. They can be narrow (for making defence easy), or wide (for making attack easy).

Narrow for making defence easy

Wide for making attack easy

A. Take a small bat and a ball which bounces well. Move around controlling the ball with downward and upward bounces.

Look for the correct grip on the bat and a fairly stiff wrist to control the height and speed of a bounce. If anyone is out of control suggest beginning with bouncing on the spot, then walking a few paces bouncing the ball, etc. Try changing the type of ball, eg larger, less or more bouncy (ie more predictable).

B. (i) With a partner. Set out a court using ropes. Decide the ball which suits you best. Play over the net space and try to keep the rally going.

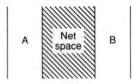

This is a co-operative practice which progresses from Year 3 Net Unit Lesson 2. Revise when to hit the ball, and encourage sideways stance. Introduce larger padder bats. Look for controlling bounces up or down before the ball is returned.

Hitting point

Send

Bounce

B. (ii) Introduce two hoops into the practice. In the diagram they are positioned for right-handers to practice forehand shots.

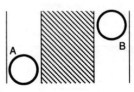

Equipment
As B(ii).

Target
To try to hit the ball so that it bounces in your partner's hoop. Controlling bounces up or down can be used to keep the rally going.

Ask
The children to adjust the positioning of the hoops so that they practice different types of shot, eg:

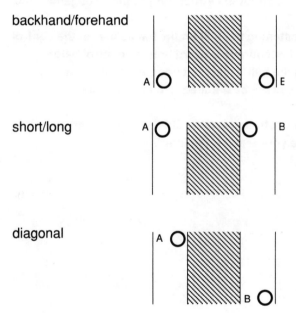

backhand/forehand

short/long

diagonal

Develop
A variety of of hoop positions. If a pair of different abilities is not succeeding in a rally, try the following:

One feeds by hand into the hoop, the other hits (five times then change). The higher achiever can attempt shots they find more challenging.

Set the hoops so that the challenge is differentiated (differentiation by task) for each child.

A. With a partner. Take a bat and a small ball. Practice rolling with bounces and controlling hits.

Experiment with different shapes and sizes of bat and ball. Make up some game rules to play by.

B. (i) With a partner. Make up a net game using any equipment where the ball must not bounce (ie through the air only) during the rally.

Allow time for practice. Ask about the decisions children are making about the structuring of their net game.

Expect catching the ball on the bat as part of the control skill, and encourage upward bounce control before sending the ball back, not continuous rallies. Ask which bat and ball are best suited to this challenge.

Use demonstrations of the children's invented games to illustrate your teaching points.

Equipment

Wire skittles, ropes and bean bags or canes for the
net, ropes for court marking.

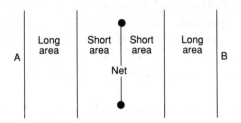

Target

To rally with your partner. The emphasis is on
co-operation, to practice skills. Introduce a high net
which allows more time for the ball to travel through
the air, giving more time for players to plan and
execute their responses, leading to better rallying.

Ask

How will you use the short and long areas? What kind
of shots will happen?

Develop

Encourage the appropriate response from the receiver
to the shot by the sender, to keep the rally going. Ask
players to develop a game, the rules of which use the
long and short areas (eg, if the ball is played into the
short area, the next shot should be played into the
long area).

Introduce sidelines using bean bags, quoits, etc to
produce a court. Rules can be agreed between
players.

A. Take a small ball. Travel around tossing the ball into the air and into a free space, let it bounce, collect the ball and repeat.

Look for use of downward cradle, underarm throwing and choosing a free space to toss the ball. Use a large space, eg netball court size.

PR – Develop catching, no bounce.

B. (i) With a partner. Stand five paces apart. Throw the ball underarm through the air to arrive at waist height.

Look for receiver watching the whole flight of the ball from the sender's hand, and making a downward catching cradle. Sender, if right-handed, left foot forward (vice-versa if left-handed), knees flexed, releasing the ball as hand points towards receiver's waist.

Return to using a bounce if catching is unsuccessful.

B. (ii) With a partner. Stand ten paces apart. Throw the ball overarm through the air to reach your partner at chest height.

The ball is held as in B(i). If the thrower is right-handed the left foot is placed forwards, the left hand pointing to the receiver (vice-versa if left-handed). The throwing arm is drawn back straight before bending as the ball is released.

Use a high trajectory at first. This allows the receiver more time to anticipate where the ball will arrive.

Receiver makes an upward cradle, arms outstretched, looking through fingers. As the ball is received the hands are brought to the chest, knees bending, to absorb the shock of the catch.

Equipment
Ropes or bean bags to mark an area, a small ball.

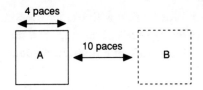

Target
A tries to throw the ball overarm into B's area. B catches the ball and throws it back.

Look for
Accurate judgment of force and trajectory. Children can be asked to judge their own actions and ask their partner for feedback. Was the throw too short or too long?

Ask
Can you invent a scoring system for this game? How can you make it more challenging or suitable for players of mixed ability?

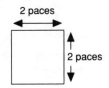

Develop
The receiver's judgement of depth. As the ball is in the air, can the receiver call 'short' or 'long' before the ball lands? Can the children invent scoring for this new game?

A. With a partner. In a space, practice underarm and overarm throwing, through the air and with a bounce.

Encourage experimentation with trajectory and use of upward and downward cradles as appropriate. Use light, small balls which are safe in a restricted space.

B. (i) With a partner. Stand eight paces apart; one ball, one padder bat. The sender (bowler) bounces the ball to arrive at waist height. The batter stands sideways to the sender and hits the ball back gently so the bowler can catch it. Change over after five hits.

Let the batter decide the best way to stand to make a hit. You can ask them to experiment with different ways, but they must stand sideways to the bowler. Ask them to think about their foot positions and their hitting arm. Is the best stance the same as that for overarm throwing?

B. (ii) With a partner. Stand six paces apart; one bat, one airflight ball. Bowler sends the ball through the air to reach the batter at waist height. Batter tries to hit the ball back over bowler's head. Change over after three hits.

Look for an accurate underarm throw. Ask the batter to watch the bowler's hand, and not to begin the hitting action until the ball has left the bowler's hand. More power can be used in hitting an airflight ball (see Year 3 Fielding Unit Lesson 4).

Non-stop Hitting   A hitting & throwing game for four/ five players.

Equipment
Two large hoops, one skittle or cone, one vinyl sponge
or airflight ball, a variety of padder bat shapes.

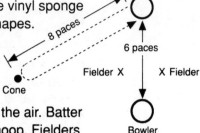

Target
Bowler sends the ball underarm through the air. Batter
hits it, runs to the cone and back to the hoop. Fielders
can prevent a score by returning the ball to the bowler
in the hoop before the batter arrives back in the hoop.
The batter cannot be stumped or caught. After five
bowls the players rotate one place anticlockwise.

Look for
Batters standing correctly to receive; bowler sending
ball at waist height; pointing to target before throwing
overarm; catching cradles being made early.

Ask
Batter: 'Where are you trying to hit the ball?' 'Which
sector is undefended?' (refer to sectors, Fielding Unit
Lesson 3). Fielders: 'Where will you stand for a right-
/left-handed batter?' 'Which type of throw is better
for a long distance?'.

Develop
Concentrate on teaching hitting. There is nothing
more frustrating than missing the ball time after time
and not knowing why. Draw the batter's attention to
the bowler's hand and remind them not to begin the hit
until the ball is released. Allow batters to choose the
bat shape which gives them the most success.

Keep the number of fielders to two, so that batters
have to make appropriate decisions about where to hit.

A. With a partner. Take three hoops (or use ropes) and some bean bags. Invent a target throwing game which you can make easier or more difficult.

B. (i) In groups of three. One ball, one rope, three cones, cricket-bat shape. Bowler bowls underarm into the rope circle placed to the batter's left (for right-handed batters); batter hits the ball through the cones to the fielder. After four hits, all children change roles.

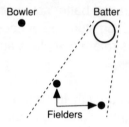

PR – Use other sectors which require different types of shot.

Encourage bowler and batter to co-operate.

Ask batter to step forwards with the front foot towards the rope as the ball is bowled, and adjust the position of the rope if necessary.

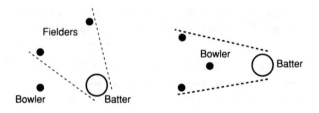

NB Similar sector games can be played with padder bats and through-the-air bowling.

Non-stop Hitting | A game for four players.

Equipment
Cricket-bat shape, airflight or vinyl-coated ball, two cones.

Fielder

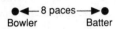
Bowler   Batter

Fielder

Target
Bowler and batter play as a team versus the two fielders. After eight hits (four each) the teams change roles.

Batter and bowler should co-operate to manage hits to undefended sectors. This means the bowler must pitch the ball in the correct place.

Ask
What strategy will the fielders use to defend? What rule will stop the batter running (eg caught out)? What will count as a score?

Develop
Concentrate on teaching the hitting action. Develop decision-making by the attacking and defensive teams.

Invasion Unit — Intended learning outcomes: PoS to be covered

Skills	Decisions/strategies
L1: Bouncing medium/large ball following a partner. Revision of bounce and chest passing, and passing and moving. Passing and following in fours. Revise **Possession 3 v 1** using hands.	**Attack 4 v 2**: introduction of four attackers v two defenders (uneven sides). Development of attack positioning and attack triangle. Use of wide court to favour attack success. Defence: person-to-person and zonal. Development of marking a person and a space.
L2: Dribbling and guarding. Use of speed and changes of direction to attack. Good footwork and anticipation to defend. Passing and signalling. **Possession 3 v 1:** concentrating on feint or dummy for attackers.	Development of person-to-person marking. Concept of keeping own body between attacker and the scoring line or goal. Introduction of second guard: 3 v 2 defenders to favour practice of person-to-person marking.
Attack: signalling, feinting, moving to free space, shooting to the goal. **Defence:** good footwork – no contact. Construct own rules for administration and conduct of the game.	**Court-End Ball 4 v 4**: with one player from each team as goal on end line. Even-sided. Attack triangle. Person-to-person defence. Test narrow and wide courts.
L3: Carrying a rugby-shape ball, dodging and weaving. Passing on the move to a partner. Passing, moving forwards into a space.	**Caught 3 v 1**: develops peripheral vision of attackers and makes defender watch/ anticipate direction of passes.
L4: Passing and travelling. Passing in threes. Revise **Attack 4 v 2** with rugby-shape ball.	**Touch and Pass 3 v 3:** Scoring along an end-line. Stepping over the ball when touched introduces the concept of on/off side. Person-to-person defence.
L5: Dribbling with feet, speeding up, slowing down with control, stopping. Revise side foot, front foot, passing, wedge trapping, outside of foot passing. **Change Ball**; **Possession 3 v 1**.	**Attack 4 v 2**: using feet. Wide pitch, large goal. Decisions as L1. Defenders mark person but no challenging/tackling at this stage.
L6: Dribbling following a partner. Trapping using chest, thigh. Throw-in to head back.	**Score:** even-sided 3 v 3 using feet. Develop positions for attack. Develop 4 v 4 with goalkeeper on wide pitch. Decisions as L1.

Invasion Unit cont   Intended learning outcomes: PoS to be covered

Skills	Decisions/strategies
L7: Unihoc dribbling around obstacles. Push-passing to a partner. Revise **Change Ball** signalling/accurate passing. Revise **Possession 3 v 1.**	**Court Unihoc 3 v 3**: as L6.

Net Unit   Intended learning outcomes: PoS to be covered

Skills	Decisions/strategies
L1: Padder bat – bouncing with control. Court rallying game using own rules. Co-operative rallying. Introduction of short-tennis plastic racquets – short-grip technique.	Decisions about starting, out-of-court, etc. **Net Attack:** designed to ask 'How can I win a rally?' (use width and depth). 'How can I not lose a rally?' (hit the ball back to the centre). Develop understanding of volley.
L2: Catching and throwing a light/ medium ball above the head. Introduction of volley skill. Partner: feed and volley.	**Volley 2 v 2**: co-operative rallying game. Children to decide rule structure. Introduce a 'moat'-type net which makes for higher trajectory rallies.

Fielding Unit   Intended learning outcomes: PoS to be covered

Skills	Decisions/strategies
L1: Underarm throwing (downward and upward cradles). Overarm throwing. In threes, bowling, throwing practice for accuracy. Practice of sector hitting: hit where the fielders are not defending.	**Sector Hitting**: Development of year 4 2 v 2 games using three sectors. Semi-circular rounders-type playing area.
L2: Rolling, retrieving, picking up, throwing.	**Non-stop Rounders:** one batter versus bowler and three fielders.
	Diamond Rounders: hitting game 4 v 4. Introduction of three bases. Taking turns to field (defence); bat (attack). Development of rule structure but opportunity to complete batting.
L3: Using cricket-bat shape. Sector hitting and catching. Introduction of bowling overarm.	**Non-stop Cricket:** four players (bowler and two fielders). Batter decides the undefended sector to hit into if appropriate. All bat, bowl and field. Circular-type playing area.

A. Find a partner and a large ball. Partner A leads, bouncing the ball, partner B follows. On the signal 'stop', change over; partner B becomes leader.

Restrict the area used for the warm-up so that the children weave in and out, using both hands for control. Ask 'follower' what they should be looking at besides the ball as they follow.

B. (i) Revise, with a partner, bounce and chest passes. See Invasion Unit Year 4 Lessons 1 and 2.

B. (ii) Revise travelling and passing.

B. (iii) Pass and follow, passing and moving to a space (practice for three players). You will need one ball and three hoops. A passes to B and runs to B's hoop. B catches the ball, passes to C, runs to C's hoop, etc.

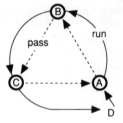

Look for accurate chest or bounce passes; catching cradles ready and turned towards passer; smooth pass and catch action as skill improves, and springy footwork.

B. (iv) Revise **Possession** 3 v 1 (Invasion Unit Year 4 Lesson 2).

Equipment

Two grids, a medium/large ball, two braids for
defenders.

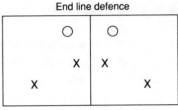

Target

Attackers have to touch the ball down on defenders'
end line to score. This is a development of **Attack**
3 v 1. The emphasis is upon learning how to attack
using attack triangles.

Ask

What positions will the attacker use?

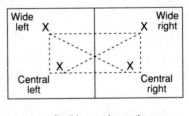

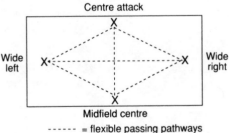

What changes in teams will be made after a score?

Develop

Defensive strategies. There are two alternatives:
person-to-person – which in this case is not possible –
or mark an area (zonal defence): one defender marks
one space, eg:

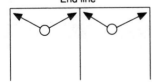

Use even sides 3 v 3 and 4 v 4.

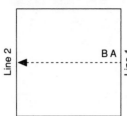

A. With a partner. One ball in a grid. A starts from line 1 and dribbles to line 2. B keeps in front, shadowing, using good footwork. When A reaches line 2, change (ie B dribbles to line 1, A defends).

Attacker in possession can use speed or direction to move defender. Defender must try to stay between the ball and the defence line, but not intercept the ball, just guard. This practice is useful for person-to-person defensive marking and emphasises no contact.

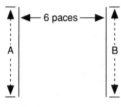

B. (i) With a partner. Stand six paces apart; one ball, four ropes. A passes to B then moves to a new space and signals with hands where they want the ball to be passed – chest, left or right side, overhead, or waist. B reads the signal and uses the appropriate pass.

Look for good footwork, accurate passes, correct cradles, and smooth take-in/give-out action. An opponent can be introduced between the passers to increase difficulty.

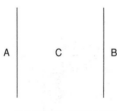

B. (ii) Guard-in-the-Middle. Four players, one ball. The three players try to make ten passes without the guard touching the ball. If the guard intercepts a pass, the player who made the intercepted pass becomes the guard; if not, the player to make the tenth pass becomes the guard.

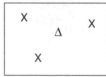

Δ guard
X passers

The emphasis is to practise feinting (any action which misleads an opponent as to the direction a pass is going to take) eg, feint upwards followed by a low pass. Feints should be made slowly to draw an opponent into making a wrong decision.

PR – Introduce a second guard (3 v 2).

Court End Ball — A passing game for 4 v 4 with side and end lines.

Equipment

Court (part of a netball court or two grids), one ball, braids for one team, four cones.

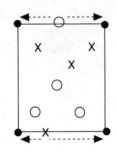

Target

To pass to a player of your own team who must be standing on the line. The player who makes the scoring pass changes with the player on the bench. The game is started with a pass from the centre.

Look for

Good examples of signalling and feinting for demonstration. Ask one group to demonstrate and ask the others to look for signalling, then feinting.

Ask

Let the children decide the rule structure. How will the game be restarted after a scoring pass? How will playing to end lines affect attack and defence tactics? Can the goalperson move along the end line?

Develop

Person-to-person marking, but emphasise that there should be no physical contact. How does an attacker escape from their marker to receive a pass? Answer: move in front, or to the side.

Emphasise to defenders to watch their opponent and the position of the ball and stay goal side.

Use a wide court instead of a long one.

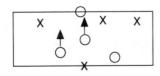

Is attack or defence more successful on a wide court?

A. Take a rugby-shape ball (or a round ball). Carry the ball in both hands and move around the space, dodging and weaving. On signal, place the ball on the ground, ie, score a try, and pick up the ball nearest to yours. Continue running and dodging until next signal.

Restrict the area. Encourage the use of both hands to hold the ball and ask the children to hold it out in front of the body as they move, to aid balance, and later, passing.

B. (i) With a partner. Stand three paces apart, facing the same way. Pass the ball sideways to each other. Begin standing still, then slowly walking forwards, then jogging.

The ball should be swung away and then towards the receiver, who makes a downward catching cradle. The swing pass reaches the receiver at waist height, and slightly in front of the body.

B. (ii) With a partner. Pass the ball to each other as you walk (jog, run) around the grid. Count the number of passes you make.

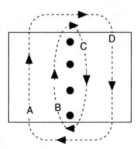

Use cones, skittles or bean bags to mark the passing lanes; four pairs can work in each grid. The ball is swung across in front of the body, to reach the receiver at waist height.

Caught	A passing and dodging game for four players.

Equipment

One 10 m x 10 m grid, a rugby ball.

X catchers
○ free runner

Target

Catchers have to pass the ball among themselves, the target being to touch the free runner with the ball. The catcher must be holding the ball in two hands when touching the ball against the free runner for the free runner to be caught. The catcher then changes with the free runner.

Look for

Secure handling, good footwork, signalling for the ball, team work to catch the free runner. Use a successful group to demonstrate good team work.

This practice develops the peripheral vision of the passers.

Ask

Will catchers be allowed to run with the ball? What tactics will you use to trap the free runner? (For example, force them out of the grid or trap them in a corner, or chase them until they are exhausted!)

Develop

Five players: four catchers, one free runner; then three catchers, two free runners. (When one free runner is caught, they join the catchers.)

A. With a partner. Jogging with a ball, passing it sideways to each other. Count how many passes you make.

Children should change sides to practice passing to the right and left. Passes should be sent at waist height and caught with two hands. The receiver's downward cradle should always be ready, ie, moving with hands in front of body. Encourage moving on curved and straight pathways.

B. (i) Groups of two or three players, one grid or two sides of the playground. Pass the ball to each other and touch the ball down on the end line to score a try. Pick up the ball and return, passing, to score at the other end.

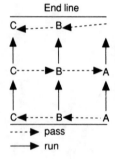

End line

---- ▶ pass

—— ▶ run

If in twos, change sides after each try so that players practice passing to the right and left. If in threes, change the centre player after each score. Look for smooth passing – receiving and giving out – which means having the catching cradle ready to receive.

B. (ii) With a partner or in threes. Same area as for B(i). A rolls out the ball, runs after it, picks it up, and passes sideways to B. B catches the pass and scores a try on the end line. Change over. If in threes, use the alternative organisation illustrated.

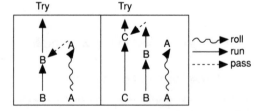

Children should bend low when scooping up the ball and try not to stop running as they make the pick-up. B and C should remain behind A to receive the sideways pass.

B. (iii) Play **Attack** 4 v 2 before even-sided **Touch and Pass**. Use **Touch and Pass** rules.

A passing game for six players (3 v 3).

Equipment

A rugby ball, braids for one team, two grids, four cones or bean bags to mark end line.

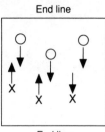

End line

End line

Target

To touch the ball down on or over the opposing team's end line to score one try. The game starts and restarts with a backwards pass from the centre. If touched by an opponent's hands whilst you are in possession, you must stop and step over the ball.

Look for

Players moving into a free space to receive a swing pass and holding the ball in both hands while dodging and weaving.

Safety: This game is not suitable for a hard surface. The end line must not be near a wall or windows.

Ask

Allow the children to decide rule structure. How is the game to be restarted after the ball goes out over the side or end line? Should you play on from a dropped pass? How many touches before possession is lost?

Develop

An understanding of passing backwards and running forwards and 'on-side' play. Stepping over should help to keep attackers and defenders on their own side.

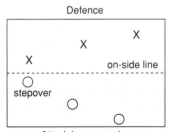

A wide grid allows attack space to dodge and run.

87

A. Take a large ball and begin dribbling anywhere in the area. Can you speed up and then slow down keeping the ball close to your feet? On the signal, can you turn using the outside of your foot? Can you stop the ball using the bottom of your foot?

When dribbling quickly ask the children to use the outside of the foot to push the ball forwards, knees flexed, keeping the ball in front of the body. Use a large area to allow for speed dribbling.

B. (i) With a partner. Stand eight paces apart. Practice side foot passing, front foot passing, and wedge trapping.

For side foot passing see Year 3, and for front foot passing see Year 4.

Progress to returning the ball without the need to trap it first, and to passing to the side of your partner so that they have to move into line to return the ball.

B. (ii) With a partner. Stand eight paces apart. Pass the ball to each other using the outside of the foot.

The kicking foot must be pointed and turned slightly to the side as the ball is hit. Ask the children to push the ball forwards with the inside of the foot and then strike it with the outside. Ask them if they can make the ball swerve using this kick.

B. (iii) Use **Change Ball** and

B. (iv) Possession games to use the increased repertoire of passing and trapping skills.

Equipment

Two grids, one ball, two braids for defenders, two cones for goals.

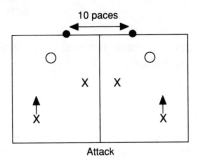

Target

For attack team to score a goal and defending team to prevent a score. Emphasise attack triangle strategy and positioning (see Lesson 1 Invasion Unit).

Ask

Children to decide rule structure. If the ball goes out at the side, should the game be restarted with a pass in or throw in? What happens after a score? How should roles rotate?

Develop

What happens to the attack if the goals are narrowed? (Corner kick for ball out over the defence end line.)

Add a goalkeeper to the defence team (four attack versus three defence).

A. Find a partner and any ball. Partner A leads, dribbling the ball with the feet, partner B follows. On the signal to stop, they change over; partner B becomes the leader.

Progress to both players with a ball. Using smaller balls provides quite a challenge!

B. (i) With a partner. Stand six paces apart, one ball between two. Send the ball with a bounce pass to reach your partner at waist height. The receiver traps the ball using the body, then returns it, under control, with the feet. Change over after three bounce passes.

The player trapping the ball uses their chest to deflect the ball downwards onto the ground. They must try to withdraw the controlling surface – chest and tummy – as the ball touches it, to take the speed from the ball so that it remains within controlling distance of the feet.

B. (ii) Use the same organisation, but try to control the ball with the thigh before returning it with the feet.

The player trapping the ball moves their thigh towards the ball so that the ball drops to the ground within controlling distance. They must be in line with the bounce pass.

B. (ii) With a partner. One partner uses a two-handed * throw-in-type feed, the other holds the ball back.

The player heading the ball must have their feet placed backwards and forwards and contact the ball on the centre of the forehead. Moving towards the ball as it is served combined with turning the neck imparts changes of direction.

* Throw-in: take ball in two hands back behind head and throw in a smooth action – release above head, extend arms.

Equipment

Two grids, one ball, four skittles, braids for one team.

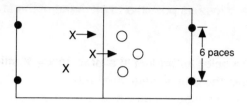

Target

To pass the ball through your opponent's goal. Start and restart at the centre. If the ball goes out of play at the side the restart should be a throw-in. There is no goalkeeper.

Look for

Calling for the ball when in a free space. Throwing-in to feet, chest, head, followed by the appropriate control.

Ask

Children to decide rule structure.

Develop

Attack triangle strategy; hide and centre positioning; person-to-person defence.

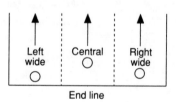

Use a wide grid; 4 v 4 with a goalkeeper. Rotate the goalkeeper after a score.

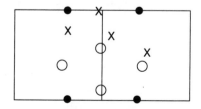

Remove the goals. Play **End Ball** rules (any ball trapped on the end line is a score; any ball headed over the end line from a throw-in or pass scores two).

A. Take a hockey-stick shape and a small ball. Dribble inside the grid avoiding the obstacles. Try to keep the ball as close as possible to the head of the stick all the time.

Place obstacles at random in a large space. Remind the children of the grip needed. For better control, the lower hand should be moved further down the stick handle. Ask if they can turn to the left and to the right.

B. (i) With a partner. One stick each, one ball between two, ten paces apart. Pass the ball to each other. Try to keep the ball on the ground.

The passer bends the knees and pushes the ball forwards (push-pass). The aim is to keep the head of the stick as close to the ground as possible. Ask the players to stop the ball before they pass it back. If the ball is being lifted, too much effort is going into the bottom (lower) hand.

PR – Use three cones to develop a passing/trapping practice.

B. (ii) Revise **Change Ball** using the above passing skills plus signalling.

B. (iii) Introduce opposition/marking with 3 v 1 **Possession**.

B. (iv) Revise 4 v 2 **Attack** using the rules from Year 5 Lesson 5.

Equipment

Four cones or skittles, a ball, six sticks, braid for one team, wide pitch (two grids).

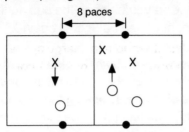

Safety: Use an airflight ball, not a hard ball.

Target

Encourage moving into a space to receive a pass. At first the children will spend a lot of time bringing the ball under control, so do not encourage tackling at this early stage. Positioning, ie playing within an area, left, right, or centre (and changing positions), might be useful to encourage more passing. Try it!

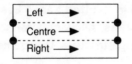

Safety: When passing or shooting, the head of the stick should be kept below waist height.

Ask

Observe how the children cope with the lack of rules. How have groups solved the problem of restarting play after a goal, after the ball has gone out over the side or end line, or after a stick has been lifted dangerously? By this stage they should be able to formulate a set of rules for any game which is played on a court.

Develop

4 v 4 on two grids. Add goalkeepers but widen goals.

A. Take a small bat and a ball which bounces well. Practice bouncing the ball on the ground and in the air. Can you bounce it on one side of the bat and then on the other? Can you balance the ball on the bat, throw the ball up, and then balance it again?

Look for the surface of the bat pointing in the direction in which the child wishes the ball to travel. Bouncing the ball on either side of the bat is asking them to use the backhand. The balancing practice makes them aware of how the angle of the bat face affects the behaviour of the ball.

B. (i) With a partner. Set up a court with a net made from skittles, ropes, canes, etc.

B. (ii) Play a game where the ball bounces on each side of the net.

B. (iii) Play a game where the ball is kept in the air.

Use skills described in Net Unit Year 4 Lessons 1 and 2. Develop backhand shots. Allow children to develop their own rules and scoring structure. Use game cards to speed up organisation.

Concentrate on co-operative rallying. Short-tennis racquets (plastic) can be introduced for these practice games.

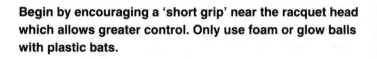

Begin by encouraging a 'short grip' near the racquet head which allows greater control. Only use foam or glow balls with plastic bats.

Equipment

Ropes, 'net' (skittles, canes, etc), bean bags to mark side of court lines, padder bats/plastic racquets, light ball.

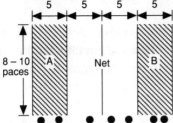

Target

To play the ball on the first bounce into the shaded target area.

This game is designed to develop the attacking strategies of depth and width after the basic skills of forehand and backhand have been practised.

Ask

How can you attack successfully (win a rally)?
Answer: Hit the ball where your opponent isn't!
How can you keep the ball in play? Where is it best to hit the ball so that you can regain the centre position on the baseline? Answer: Hit the ball back to the centre of the baseline and position yourself in the centre of your own baseline to receive. This defensive tactic denies the attacker the best or widest angle of attack.

Develop

The understanding of attack and defence using width and depth.

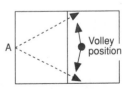

Hitting the ball in the air close to the net (volley) may be used as a tactic to win the rally. The same principle of attack applies: bisect the angle and keep close to the net.

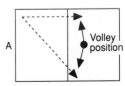

A. Take a light, medium or large ball, or a large foam ball and practice throwing and catching the ball using an upward cradle, but don't let the ball drop below head height.

This is a basic introduction to volleyball-type skill (volley). Try to bend the elbows, holding the ball on fingertips, before pushing it into the air again. A light ball is essential for this practice.

PR – Travel around the space keeping the ball above head height. Begin walking; keep an eye on the ball and on free spaces.

B. (i) With a partner. Six paces apart. Partner A feeds the ball underarm, partner B volleys the return. Change after four returns.

The feed should be high, dropping onto the head of the feeder.

PR – Introduce a hoop as a target for the volleyer.

Equipment
One grid, ropes or bean bags, a light foam ball.

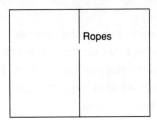

Target
To keep the ball in the air for as long as possible. Try to beat your own record.

Safety: A foam ball builds confidence.

This is a co-operative rallying game. Allow children to pass to their own side before sending the ball over the net. Catching and holding the ball is allowed.

Ask
How will you start the rally? Where and how will you stand to receive the serve (start)? How will you work as teams of two and four to keep the ball in the air?

Develop
Make the net a moat-type which makes for higher trajectory shots.

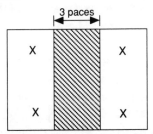

Add a skittle and cane net or use ropes tied to netball posts and a fence to increase height (if available).

A. Take a small ball. Toss the ball underarm high into the air above your head, and catch it as it falls. Try several different types of ball.

After the ball is thrown the catcher should leave the arms outstretched, looking through an upward catching cradle at the ball. As soon as the ball touches the fingers, the arms should bend to absorb the shock of catching the ball. Bending the knees also helps.

B. (i) With a partner. Stand ten paces apart, one ball between two. Send the ball underarm through the air to each other. Count the number of catches you make.

The sender should be pointing at the target with the non-throwing hand. Make sure the receiver is showing an upward catching cradle before the ball is thrown. Emphasise this as an important safety point.

PR – If children make a successful catch they should step one pace backwards; one pace forwards if unsuccessful. Use different types of 7 cm ball.

B. (ii) With a partner. Stand ten paces apart. The sender throws the ball underarm, the receiver sends it back overarm. Change over after five throws.

This practice requires the receiver of the underarm throw to make a downward catching cradle and the receiver of the overarm throw an upward cradle.

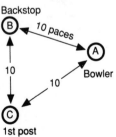

Backstop
B
10 paces
A
10
10 Bowler
C
1st post

B. (iii) In threes with three large hoops. A sends the ball underarm to B, who throws overarm to C, who throws overarm to A. After three turns, move round one place anticlockwise. Make sure everyone is using the correct cradle, and turns to face in the direction from which the ball will come. This is the basic rounders triangle, bowler (A), backstop (B), first post (C).

Sector Hitting: fielding practices based on the sectors associated with rounders-type games.

Examples of game cards

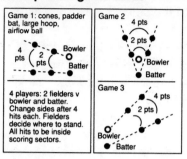

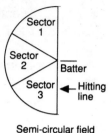

Semi-circular field

Progress to using these skills in a small-sided game where attack and defence decisions can be made.

Non-stop Rounders

A catching and throwing game for five players.

Equipment

Two large hoops, one cone or skittle, one airflight ball, one small bat.

Target

Batter receives five underarm bowls. To score, batter runs to cone and returns before fielders throw ball back to bowler. Batter cannot be stumped or caught, and receives all five bowls before players move round one place anticlockwise.

Look for

Batter standing sideways to receive, moving front foot in direction of hit; backstop standing to side to which bowler will bowl (the side batter is holding bat); fielders having cradles ready, returning ball overarm. Deciding which sector to defend.

Ask

Where will the fielders stand for each batter? Why?
Safety: Do not use a hard ball or tennis ball.

A. With a partner. One ball between two. Start the practice side by side. Partner A rolls the ball out gently, runs after it, scoops it up, turns, throws overarm to B, and runs back to the start. B rolls the ball, etc.

Ask the children to try to overtake the ball before it stops rolling, bend the knees, and using one hand, fingers pointing to the ground, scoop the ball up with a backward swing of the arm, turn and throw.

B. (i) With a partner. One tennis or rounders ball and a hoop. Bowler bowls three balls underarm to the right of the hoop, then three to the left for the backstop to field. Change places.

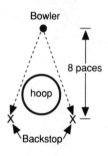

Bowler

8 paces

hoop

Backstop

The bowler should be bending the knees as they deliver the ball to reach backstop at waist height. Ask them to watch where each ball reaches the backstop (eg, if too high release the next ball a little lower). The backstop makes a downward cradle, stands to the side to which the bowler is bowling, and returns the ball overarm.

B. (ii) With a partner. Stand ten paces apart, one tennis ball between two. Roll the ball along the ground to your partner, who scoops it up and rolls it back.

The fielder should have one knee on the floor, body at a right angle to the direction of the roll, hands in a downward cradle (see illustration). This fielding position ensures that if the hands miss the ball, the legs and body will stop it.

PR – Try hands behind head, just stopping the ball with the knee. Roll the ball to left or right of your partner.

NB These practices are suitable for all fielding-type games.

Diamond Rounders | A hitting, catching & throwing game for 4 v 4.

Equipment

Four bats, four cones or skittles, two large hoops, one airflight ball.

Safety: Batter must wait well away from batting hoop to avoid being hit by the ball or a dropped bat!

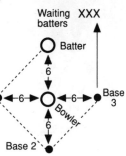

Target

Batter must hit ball and reach base three before bowler, in hoop, receives ball from fielders, to score one rounder. Each batter receives three bowls in turn, then teams change. No one can be stumped or caught out – only prevented from scoring.

Look for

Accurate underarm bowling; correct hitting stance; arm action and footwork; accurate overarm return throwing.

Ask

Where will fielders stand for each batter? Will you use a backstop?

Develop

Increase distance between bases as skill increases.

Introduce stopping at bases. Ask children to develop rules for this.

The batter should stand as for an overarm throw, weight on rear foot, beginning hitting action as bowler releases the ball. Encourage hitting by unbending the arm fast as in overarm throwing action.

Ask batters who miss why they think it happened. Did they begin the hitting action too soon (before bowler released ball)? Direct their attention to bowling hand. Build batting confidence by using a padder pat and a 9 cm ball, then padder bat and 7 cm ball; rounders bat and 9 cm ball, then rounders bat and 7 cm ball.

A. In threes.Take a cricket-bat shape, two bean bags and a rope. A bowls to B who gives a catch to C.

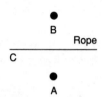

Ask the children to adjust the rope so that the ball bounces near it and it is in the best position for the batter to give a catch. Rotate positions.

PR – Change position of fielder to different sectors.

B. (i) With a partner. Stand ten paces apart, bowl the ball overarm to your partner so that it bounces once.

The ball is gripped as for an overarm throw, and the stance is sideways to the receiver, weight on the rear foot. The ball hand is held near to the chest, the other pointing at the receiver. Slowly uncurl the arm, beginning downwards and then straightening to release the ball when overhead. As the bowling arm comes over, the bowler steps forwards.

B. (ii) Play the game in A using overarm bowling. Use a hoop or a rope circular target if necessary.

Equipment
Two cones, one airflight ball, one cricket-bat shape.

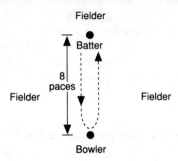

Safety: Do not use a hard ball for this game.

Target
For the batter to score as many runs between the cones as possible in five bowls. Runs may be prevented by the fielders returning the ball to the bowler. Move round one place anticlockwise after five bowls.

Look for
Underarm or overarm bowling action; correct batting technique; fielders alert to catches, catching cradles ready.

Ask
What will be counted as a run; one way or out and back? What else could stop a run (a catch, or ball hits the wicket)?

Develop
Increase the distance between batter and bowler; use a glow ball on a larger space.

Invasion Unit   Intended learning outcomes: PoS to be covered

Skills	Decisions/strategies
L1: Footwork practice, including pivoting. Bouncing ball and pivoting to change pathway. **Change Ball** with pivoting and passing. Guarding practice in threes. Revision of **Attack 4 v 2**.	**Court End Ball 4 v 4** (3 v 4 or 4 v 5). Scoring players joins own player on end line, reducing the sides, thus producing an advantage for the team which was scored against. Attack triangle. Person-to-person guarding .
L2: Footwork following and pivoting. **Possession 3 v 1** using pivoting. **Possession 3 v 2** practising guarding skills.	**Attack 3 v 2**: uneven-sided progression from 4 v 2. Introduction of attack strategy of wall pass to create a free player. Game structure = game –> practice skill –> game.
L3: Change Ball chest and bounce passing. Overhead pass. **Tower Ball** Principle of what do you do after possession is lost (or regained)?	**Zonal**: defending a space-type defence. **Court ball 4 v 4** or 5 v 5. Introduction of restricted spaces for scoring. **Attack**: positional play (scoring decisions). **Defence**: zonal (based on attack positions).
L4: Swing passing on the move (rugby-ball shape). Travelling forwards; passing sideways in threes; roll, pick up, pass, touch down. Introduction of rugby-type wall pass – the loop – without opposition in threes.	With opposition: teaches attacker when to release the ball when challenged and teaches the team how to create an 'overlap' or free player.
L4: Heel ball back when touched. Development of on-side understanding. Development of throw-ins from sideline.	**Touch and Backward Pass 3 v 3** or 4 v 4. **Attack**: running into space; supporting players behind ball carrier. Rules for restarting play.
L5: Dribbling and guarding (using feet). Changes of direction: chest, thigh trapping; 'chipping' for trapping. Passing skills revised, stationary and moving. Revise **Attack 3 v 2**.	Revise concept of wall pass. **End Ball 3 v 3** using feet. Wide pitch. **End Ball 4 v 4**: introduce goals as targets.

Invasion Unit cont   Intended learning outcomes: PoS to be covered

Skills	Decisions/strategies
L6: Dribbling and challenging for the ball. Side foot tackle; use of correct foot to tackle. Shooting in twos. Shooting with a goalkeeper in threes. Heading practice in twos and fours.	**Head Score 4 v 4**: headed goals score more! Introduction of restricted area for defence and attack. Even-sided games for feet and head. Decisions as L1, L2.
L7: Unihoc dribbling. **Change Ball.** Passing and shooting with and without goalkeeper. Play **Attack 3 v 2**. Practice wall pass strategy.	**Court Hockey 4 v 4** or 5 v 5 with restricted goal area. Decisions as L1, L2.

Net Unit   Intended learning outcomes: PoS to be covered

Skills	Decisions/strategies
L1: Rallying practice: forehand and backhand; short and long shots. Development of drop and lob shots. Revision of volley strategy. Develop use of shuttlecocks; through-the-air rallying.	Width and depth understanding. Appropriate decision-making depending on position of opponent. Play 1 v 1. Develop 2 v 2.
L2: Volleying practice using medium/large ball with hands. Introduction of 'dig' technique. Underarm/overarm serve. Serve/volley rallies. Revise 2 v 2 rallying game.	**Volley 3 v 3**: introduce serve to begin game; introduce rotation of positions on regaining the serve; introduce attack strategies of placing the ball in undefended spaces.

Fielding Unit   Intended learning outcomes: PoS to be covered

Skills	Decisions/strategies
L1: Underarm bowling for accuracy. Overarm throwing for distance and accuracy. Revise catching cradles. Fielding skills. Sector hitting practices.	Three sectors: semi-circular playing area: **Diamond Rounders**; **Square Rounders 5 v 5**. Decisions as year 5.
L2: Bowling overarm. Fielding and hitting (with a cricket-bat shape). Sector-hitting: circular playing area. Batter and bowler co-operate against two fielders.	Development of sectors **behind** the batter. Introduction of idea of inner and outer fielding area. **Circular Cricket 2 v 2 v 2**: developed in competitive 1 v 5 fielding game.

A. Jog, dodging and weaving, and on signal, stop with one foot in front of the other. Turn, keeping your rear foot on the floor and jog off on a new pathway.

Restrict the area used. Ensure that when stopping the children bend the leading knee. Ask them not to drag the rear foot as they stop, or when they turn (pivot).

B. (i) Take a large ball and move around bouncing the ball anywhere in the grid. On the signal, catch the ball, keeping your rear foot still, pivot and continue bouncing along the new pathway you have chosen.

The children should have the ball well under control so that most of their attention can be directed to watching others as they dodge and weave, and listen for the pivot signal.

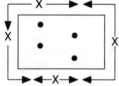

B. (ii) Progress to **Change Ball** using chest and bounce passes, and pivoting when exchanging the ball.

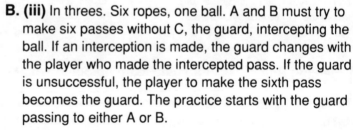

B. (iii) In threes. Six ropes, one ball. A and B must try to make six passes without C, the guard, intercepting the ball. If an interception is made, the guard changes with the player who made the intercepted pass. If the guard is unsuccessful, the player to make the sixth pass becomes the guard. The practice starts with the guard passing to either A or B.

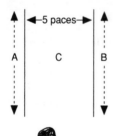

This practice teaches guarding. The guard should stand with arms spread to either side, ready to cover passes to right or left (or higher or lower). Teach the guard to watch the ball not the sender's eyes! Restrict overhead passes to help the defender.

Attack 4 v 2

A passing and positioning game for six players (see Invasion Unit Year 5 Lesson 1).

Court End Ball

An invasion game for eight players using hands, which starts even sided and progresses to uneven sides (3 v 4 or 4 v 5).

Equipment

Two grids, one ball, braids for one team.

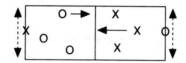

Target

To get the ball to your team's player on the end line. Score one goal each time. The scoring player then joins the player on the end line. Thus the scoring team has fewer players. Stop game and restart when 1 v 1.

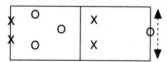

Practice attack triangle strategies, guarding skills and positioning (see Year 5 Invasion lessons).

Ask

Children to decide rule structure and scoring system and any further rules which will make the game fairer so that each team has a challenge.

Insist on no physical contact, and encourage players to use pivoting as a way of overcoming efficient guarding. Rotate the teams so that they play new opponents, eg, one court clockwise.

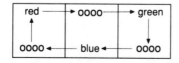

A. With a partner. Travel around the grid, one partner leading, the other following. On signal to stop, try to keep the rear foot still, and pivot. Now the lead has changed, carry on jogging.

The children should be travelling on the balls of their feet, knees bending to dodge and weave and stop. Develop this warm-up by using a ball each with the same organisation.

B. (i) Play **Possession** (3 v 1) using pivoting skill for attackers.

B. (ii) Play **Possession** but increase the defenders to two   (ie 3 v 2). Ask the attack what strategies they will adopt to keep possession. Ask defenders how they will defend.

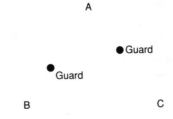

This practice increases the opposition. The attackers have to be quick to move into free positions.

Equipment
Two grids, two braids for defenders, one ball.

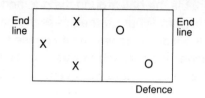

Target
For attack team (X) to get the ball to any attacker (who must be standing on the defence's end line).

This is an opportunity to teach a skill inside a game context. In this situation the defence can easily stifle the attack by marking the two players not in possession. Ask for ideas then introduce the idea of a wall pass, where the attacker in possession passes, then follows the pass, creating a free player. The other attacker can take the second defender to a free space, creating space for the passer. The attack triangle can be maintained with a number of these passes.

If this skill cannot be learned in a game situation with opposition, practice without opposition, then restart the game.

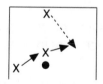

Use a cone as a defender and stand by its side. Step in front as the pass is made. Practice both sides of the court.

This skill is appropriate to all invasion-type games.

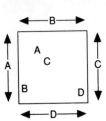

A. With a partner. Five pairs to a grid. Players in the grid have a ball and are paired with players on the sideline. Dribble the ball around the grid and on signal, stop, pivot towards your partner, pass the ball, and follow it to the sideline to which you passed. Your partner catches the ball and moves into the grid. Repeat.

The players on the sidelines can move position along the lines, so partners have to spot them and use a pass which avoids anyone in the way.

PR – Partners on the outside give the signal to change. Both partners have a ball.

B. (i) With a partner. Stand five paces apart. Hold the ball above your head, then pass the ball through the air to your partner to arrive at chest height.

The sender's arms are held straight above the head and slightly in front of the body, fingers behi.1d the ball. The wrists are moved downwards to propel the ball to the target. The receiver makes an upward catching cradle and returns the ball with a bounce or chest pass. After five passes, change over.

B. (ii) Play **Tower Ball** (six players (4 v 2)). Passers try to hit the cone; the guards try to prevent this happening.

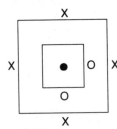

X Guards
O Attackers

Let the children make up their own rules. Ask, 'When will you change the guards?' 'What happens if a guard intercepts a pass?' 'How will the game start?' 'What type of passes will you use?'. Guards work together defending a zone (not person-to-person marking).

Equipment

Two grids with chalked semi-circles at either end, one ball, braids for one team.

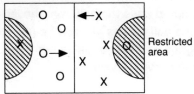

Target

To get the ball to the player of your own team standing in the semi-circle; score one goal.

Look for

The skills which have been practised: feinting and when to use it; pivoting and when to use it; dribbling and when to use it; overhead passing and guarding without physical contact with another player.

Rules to govern this type of game should now be established as necessary for the enjoyment of the game. Encourage good conduct without the need for a referee. If you see a particular aspect that needs clarification, stop the games and ask the children to make a decision on it, eg, 'What is the rule about a defender going inside the restricted area?'

Ask

What shooting trajectory scores most easily?

Develop

Two players on each team could be designated shooters; the successful shooter changes place, after a score, with the player who supplied the pass.

Attacking and defensive tactics. Attacking (positional play); defensive (zonal defence). If the ball is lost by the attack, defend spaces as the team retreats. Guard any attacker who comes into your defensive zone.

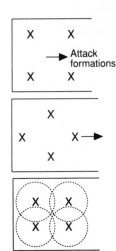

A. With a partner. Take a ball between two and practice passing to each other using sideways 'swing' passes.

The children should pass the ball from the left- and right-hand side so the ball arrives at waist height. Restrict the area to a few grids or a part of the playground. Expect some pairs to jog around passing.

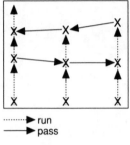

B. (i) In groups of three or four. One grid, or sides of the playground. Pass the ball down the line and back again as you jog forwards. Count how many passes you can make before reaching the end line. Can you improve on this score?

run
pass

Passes should be sent slightly backwards. Players should be fairly close together. The centre player changes at the end of each trip.

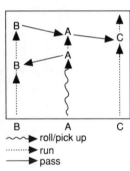

B. (ii) The same organisation as above. A rolls out the ball a little way, runs after it, scoops it up and then passes to B or C, who passes the ball to A. Repeat.

roll/pick up
run
pass

This practice is designed to help players keep behind the ball carrier, and to continue a passing movement from side to side. B and C should be slightly behind A as they follow the rolling ball; after passing, A must stay behind B or C to take the return pass. Change centre player after two trips.

B. (iii) In groups of three. A in possession jogs forward, passes to B and follows the ball behind B. A receives the ball from B and passes to C who touches down at the end of the grid.

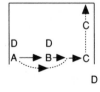

B. (iv) Practice this skill (three attack v two defence). It is the rugby equivalent of the 'wall pass' attack play. C should be released. Feed to score a try as A runs round B to form the extra person.

Equipment

Four grids (half a netball court), one ball, braids for one team.

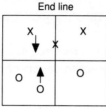

Target

To touch the ball down over your opponents' end line. After a score the game restarts with a centre pass. If touched by an opponent's hand while in possession you must stop and step over the ball.

Look for

Swing passes, and encourage the players to pass before they are touched, to ensure a more flowing game. The player running with the ball should run forwards and be touched, rather than backwards, away from opponents. The other players in the team remain behind to support the ball-carrier.

Ask

What rules are necessary to play this game? What should you do about dropped passes or opponents who obstruct to prevent a backward pass?

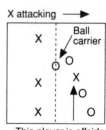

Develop

Good support play. Ask the player who is touched while in possession to put the ball on the floor and step over it. A player on the same side must then pass the ball to continue play. Teams must keep on their own side (to demonstrate the concept of off/on side).

Develop strategies for bringing the ball into play from the sideline, eg introduce a four-touch rule (possession changes if the team does not score).

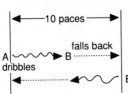

A. With a partner. One ball between two, working between two lines about ten paces apart. A dribbles the ball and B falls back, trying to keep between the ball and the end line, shadowing or guarding.

A dribbles the ball using feet in a straight pathway at first, then varies in an attempt to deceive B. Change places at the end line.

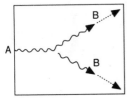

PR – A has the ball in the centre of the grid and moves forwards before dribbling to the left or right corner of the grid. B falls back shadowing A to the corner; change over.

The shadow must concentrate on the ball-carrier's feet in order to anticipate the change of direction. Springy footwork is essential if the shadow is to remain in balance.

B. (i) With a partner. Stand eight paces apart. Revise side foot passing, front foot passing, outside foot passing. Remember to trap the ball before returning it.

Encourage the use of the left and right foot to pass the ball, and develop passing without the need to trap first.

PR – Use passes moving forwards into space.

B. (ii) With a partner. Stand six paces apart. Bounce the ball to reach your partner at waist or chest height. The receiver traps it, then returns the ball to the sender. After five passes, change over.

The player trapping the ball should use the chest, stomach or thigh to deflect the ball downwards to within controlling distance of the feet before returning it with a pass. It is essential to be behind the line of the ball.

PR – Feeding with feet; chipping the ball upwards by striking the ball with a wedge action.

Play **Attack 3 v 2**. Use wall pass as in Year 6, Lesson 2, and practice to develop the skill.

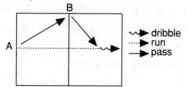

End Ball

A passing and marking game for six players (3 v 3).

Equipment

One ball, braids, four grids (wide pitch).

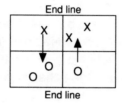

Target

To trap the ball anywhere on your opponent's end line and score one goal. Tackling is not allowed.

Each player must mark one member of the opposing team; they are not permitted to shadow anyone else.

Look for

Good footwork; passing and dribbling to beat marking players; use of wall pass.

Ask

How can you get free from your shadow? What are the rules which will govern play? How will infringements, eg, a tackle, be dealt with?

Develop

Increase the sides to 4 v 4. Introduce goals on the end lines. The object now is to score between the cones. Use goalkeepers, but decide when they will change with an outfield player. The width of the goals can be reduced to make scoring more difficult.

A. Intercept. The class is divided into two groups, each group in one half of a netball court, or four grids, one ball each. Each player dribbles the ball inside the area. Any other player can kick your ball out of the grid. If this happens you must retrieve your own ball before rejoining the game.

Use any sized ball. Challenging for the ball, or tackling has not been emphasised because it favours defence in foot activities. This practice introduces challenging for the ball. Emphasise using the side of the foot.

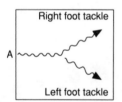

B. (i) With a partner. One ball between two, working between two lines ten paces apart. A dribbles the ball and B falls back keeping between the ball and the end line, shadowing and then challenging for the ball.

Encourage tackling with the side of the foot (from an on-balance stance) – usually the dominant foot at first.

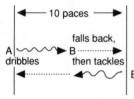

B. (ii) A dribbles straight, then to left corner; B challenges with right foot. A dribbles to right corner; B challenges with left foot.

B. (iii) With a partner. One ball between two, working across two grids (two cones needed). Push the ball forwards then shoot, using the front of your foot, through the cones to your partner. Repeat.

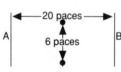

Players should strike the ball on the front of their kicking foot, so they must point their toes and look down at the ball to keep the shot low. Receiver stops the ball with their hands, or traps it.

A   B   C

PR – In threes. Two grids, two cones. A has the ball and shoots. B is goalkeeper. If the ball is saved, B rolls the ball to C, who shoots. Rotate positions after two shots each.

B. (iv) With a partner. One ball between two, stand six
paces apart. A serves the ball underarm, B heads it
back to chest, feet, then head. Change over.

Look for
An underarm throw which is not too low. The feet of
the person heading the ball should be backwards and
forwards, knees flexed, eyes on the ball.

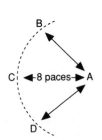

**PR – Pressure heading. One ball between four. C feeds ball
to A who heads to B or D. Change over after eight headers.
Look for headers to suit feed height, and when the ball is
struck, knees straightening, to impart force to the header.**

C. (i) A heading and passing game for 3 v 3, 4 v 4, or
3 v 4 players, using one ball, braids, two grids.

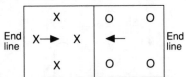

Target
To head the ball over, or trap the ball on, the
opposition's end line. Any ball out at the side causes a
throw in. Headers can be defended only with the head.

C. (ii) A heading and passing game for 5 v 5 players,
using four grids, ropes or bean bags.

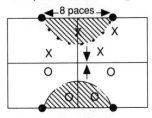

Target
To shoot or head the ball through the opponent's
goals. Only one person in each team can handle the
ball at any one time, in the restricted area.

Children to decide the rule structure for each game.

A. With a partner. A ball and unihoc stick each, A leading, B following. On the signal, both stop and trap the ball; A passes to B, B passes to A and B leads.

Look for close control; develop short passes.

B. (i) Change Ball
A game for eight players (four pairs).

Equipment
Four balls, one grid (chalked/marked with bean bags).

Target
Players dribble with a ball in the grid anywhere until the signal, then they stop and push-pass to the partner on the sideline. Players change over.

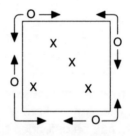

Look for stick heads kept below waist height and the ball passed smoothly along the ground. The push-pass should be a sideways action, feet well apart and the knees bent.

B. (ii) Use B(i) and (ii), Lesson 6 with unihoc stick.

B. (iii) Use B(iii), Lesson 6 to develop unihoc shooting skill.

Aim: to keep the ball low. How will you accomplish this? How will you keep the stick action safe?

B. (iv) Use 3 v 2 as in other invasion units. Practice wall pass with or without opposition.

Equipment

Four grids with chalked or bean-bag-marked semi-circles, or a netball court, one ball, four cones, eight sticks, braids.

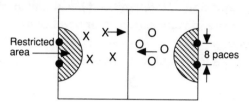

Target

To get the ball through the opponent's goal. Score one goal. No players, except goalkeepers, may enter the restricted areas (the semi-circles).

Look for

Calling for the ball when ready to receive a pass. Person-to-person marking and shadowing. Attack triangle tactics as adopted in other ball games.

Safety: Sticks must not be raised above waist height.

Ask

Should the team have positions? When should the goalkeeper be changed? How is the game started and restarted after a goal? What happens if the ball goes out at the side or end line? Will tackling be allowed?

Develop

Positional attacking play; person-to-person and zonal defensive play.

A. With a partner. Set up a net and a court. Use large padder or short-tennis-type racquets and a sponge or glow ball. Practice rallying for depth and width.

Encourage revision of forehand and backhand shots and correct timing and stance. (See Year 5 Net Unit).

B. (i) Set up a four-section court using ropes or cones.

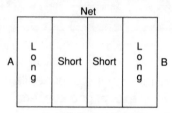

Ask, 'What happens if you hit the ball into the short area?', 'What happens if your opponent hits the ball into the short area?'. Answer: drop shots and lobs are the consequence.

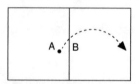
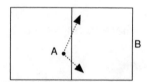

A's decision is lob   A's decision is drop shot

Take these shots out of the game context and practice them using hoops as targets. Return to the game when proficient. Such a process builds an understanding of when to use the strategy in a game situation.

B. (ii) Ask 'When can you volley the ball?', 'Where do you need to stand to intercept?'.

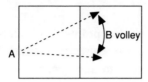

Answer: Volleyers position themselves close to the net to intercept, thus reducing the space available to the attacker.

Ask

How will you return the ball if you are at the back of the court and the volleyer has the net covered? Answer: With a lob or passing shot.

B. (iii) Revise these strategies and the principle of depth and width in a full-court situation. Teach appropriate decision-making as well as the skills and techniques involved.

Develop

A 2 v 2 game in a modified form, from co-operative rallying to competitive play.

The same principles apply to through-the-air net games like badminton.

A. With a partner. Practice volleying a large/medium ball to each other. See how many times you can keep the ball in the air.

For basic volley teaching points see Year 5 Net Unit Lesson 2 Section A. Concentrate on attempting to take in and give out in one continuous action (volley). Keep the trajectory high.

B. (i) With a partner. Six paces apart, partner A feeds the ball underarm, partner B returns the ball with a 'dig' action. Change over after four returns.

The contact area is the inside of the forearm. The elbows do not bend, but pivot from the shoulder; use the knees to lift into the action. Use a soft sponge ball for this practice.

PR – Introduce a hoop as a target for the sender. One partner volleys, one digs.

B. (ii) With a partner. Experiment with ways of serving the ball to each other accurately.

Underarm serve: use the heel of the hand.

Overarm serve: use the open palm of the hand. Keep the thumb to one side.

B. (iii) Practice, with a partner, a serve followed by a volleying rally.

C. (i) Volley a 2 v 2 net game (see Year 5 Net Unit Lesson 2).

C. (ii) Volley a 3 v 3 net game.

Target

Introduce a serve to begin the game. Ask the children to structure the rules.

Develop

Introduce basic rotation of players' positions when appropriate, eg when a side serves:

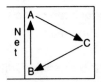

A. With a partner. One ball between two. Stand eight paces apart, throwing underarm to each other so the ball arrives between hand and knee height. Move 15 paces apart, practice overarm throwing to each other. Progress from light ball to tennis ball.

B. (i) In fours. One ball, four large hoops. A throws underarm to B, who throws overarm to C. C throws overarm to D, who returns the ball to A. Rotate one position anticlockwise after four circuits.

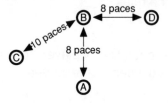

This is a rounders practice for bowler, backstop and first and fourth bases. Look for ready catching cradles and accurate throwing through the air.

B. (ii) Revise B(ii), Year 5 Fielding Unit Lesson 2 .

PR – With a partner. Stand 15 paces apart and roll the ball to each other. The receiver moves forward to meet the ball, and, using a downward cradle, bends to scoop the ball up before rolling it back. Repeat. Receiver should put one foot towards the ball and try to scoop it up in front of that foot.

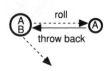

B. (iii) With a partner, in a hoop. One tennis or rounders ball. A rolls the ball out, runs after it, scoops it up and throws it overarm to B. A returns to the hoop. B rolls the ball out in a new direction to begin again.

Look for correct catching cradles, and scooping the ball up with a backward swing of the arm, before turning, pointing and throwing overarm.

B. (iv) Revise **Non-stop Rounders**, Year 5 Fielding Unit Lesson 1.

Square Rounders   A fielding game for 5 v 5 players.

Equipment

Six cones, a large hoop
(or make bowler's square from
ropes) a light ball, a variety of
padder bats.

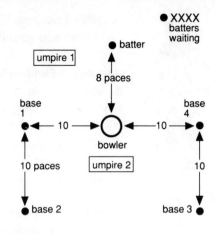

Target

To score a rounder by reaching
base four without being caught
or stumped. Batters may stop at
any base. Each batter receives
three bowls. If out, they go to the
back of the batting line, but still
receive the remaining bowls. When all batters have
received three bowls, the teams change.

Look for

Accurate bowling and concentrate on teaching
successful hitting. The batter should not begin the
hitting action until the ball has left the bowler's hand.
They can then decide if the hit was too early or too late
and adjust.

Ask

Fielders to return the ball quickly to the bowler, to stop
the batters running around the square. Remind batters
to run outside the posts and to remain in contact with
them while waiting. The bowler should place the
fielders for each batter: left- or right-handed? Hitting
power? What will be judged as out?

Develop

Children can umpire their own games. Umpire 1
decides if the ball height is correct as it reaches the
batter. It must be between the top of the head and the
knee. Umpire 2 decides on the straightness of the
bowl. It must be delivered to the batter's hitting side.

A. With a partner. Stand 12 paces apart. Bowl the ball overarm to your partner so that it bounces once.

See Year 5 Fielding Unit Lesson 3 for explanation of bowling technique. Develop by using ropes as markers; ask bowlers to jog to the rope before delivering the ball.

B. (i) With a partner. Stand ten paces apart, one tennis ball between two. Roll the ball along the ground to your partner, who scoops it up and rolls it back.

fielder

A |◄─ 8 paces ─► ● B fielder

fielder

B. (ii) In groups of five. One bat, one airflight ball, one rope, one cone. A bowls underarm to B, who hits the ball to the fielders, who return it to A. After five bowls the players rotate anticlockwise.

Revise the correct grip (see Year 5). Batters should watch the whole flight of the ball and not begin the hitting action too early. They should stand sideways to the bowler, feet slightly apart, and step forwards as they bring the bat down to strike the ball. The bowler must bowl straight and well up to the batsman. A target area could be provided.

A |◄─ 6 paces ─► ▨ B

target area ─► ▨

B. (iii) Sector hitting – cricket type

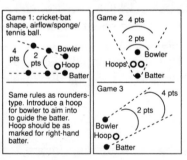

These cards are useful for organising class groups.

These sectors are not the only ones used in a cricket-type game where the playing area is circular.

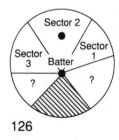

Devise a practice, using a target hoop similar to those above, but using the two new sectors.

Equipment

Cricket-bat shape, small ball, bean bags to mark inner circle, six cones for wickets, four grids for playing area.

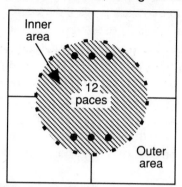

A and B: batter and bowler (six balls each).
C and D: inner area fielding team.
E and F: outer area fielding team.

Target

For the bat and bowl team to score as many runs as possible. C and D can field only in the inner area (eg backstop). E and F can field only in the outer area.

This game introduces the concept of close fielders, but still preserves the tactical co-operation between batter and bowler.

Ask

What will happen if a batter is caught or bowled?

Develop

This game can be played on an individual or competitive basis: one batter versus five fielders.

The National Curriculum key stage 2 specific programme of study describes athletic activities as 'basic actions in running ... throwing and jumping.' Adult versions which readily spring to mind are javelin, discus, 200 m sprint, high jump, pole vault. These events, requiring specialised techniques, are obviously inappropriate to the experience and physical maturity of children at key stage 2. Modified adult versions are undesirable because they assume a 'top-down' model of learning. For example, long jumping: make the run-up shorter, the pit smaller and expect the children to perform the whole skill before they have learned the principles of a range of jumping actions.

This section is based upon the principle that primary-aged children need a wide variety of jumping, running and throwing experiences before they can begin to refine the skills needed for specific athletic events (key stage 3).

The teaching of athletics skills

A. Lesson structure
(i) Introductory activity/warm up
A vigorous footwork activity, usually emphasising the contrast between running for speed (sprinting action) and running over longer distances (jogging action), or running and jumping actions and combinations. Activities * in the games skills sections are suitable athletic warm-up activities for the whole class.

(ii) Introduction or development of individual or partner or group skills
One or two skills (from running, jumping or throwing activities) for the whole class.

(iii) Group activities
Practice of skills introduced (and developed in later lessons). The emphasis is on improvement of individual performance. Children can record their own and others' performances. Groups rotate around several activities.

(iv) Concluding activity/warm-down
Group relay-type activities may be used.

B. The teaching strategies found in the sections
Observation, and task-setting and guidance in the games skills teaching section are appropriate to athletics.

C. Participation
The principle of maximising the activity and involvement of all children also applies to athletics. However, many athletic activities are strenuous and younger children may need short rest/recovery periods (they can take turns recording a partner's performance).

Try to organise group activities so that very strenuous running is followed by a contrasting run, jump or throwing activity.

The purpose of teaching athletic activities is to include all children; traditional high-jumping activities which exclude some children are not included.

D. Group activity organisation
The following units of work are for five groups of mixed ability and consist of six sessions. Each session can be the basis for several lessons. Two methods of organisation can be used:

(i) A variety of running, jumping, throwing activities eg:

Week		1	2	3		4	5	6	
Introduction		Running activities	→	→		→	→	→	
Skills (class)		Type of jumping 1→1, 1→2, 2→2	Throwing overarm	Relay (shuttle type)		Throwing push⎫ sling⎭	Hurdling	Relay (traditional pass it on)	
Group activities (five groups)	1	40 m straight or 40 m shuttle	Overarm throw	3 steps hops	G R O U P R E L A Y S	Zig-zag or compass run	Vertical jump	Hurdle	G R O U P R E L A Y S
	2	2 → 2 and 1 → 2 jump	Potato run	40 m run		Sling 1 hand or 2 hands	Pushing	Zig-zag run	
	3	Overarm throw 1 hand standing	3 steps 3 hops	2→2, 2→1		Vertical jump	Hurdling	Sling	
	4	Potato shuttle run	40 m run	Overarm throw		Push sitting 2 hand & 1 hand	Zig-zag run	Vertical jump	
	5	3 steps and 3 hops	2→2, 1→2 jump	Potato race		Hurdling	Slinging	Push	

(Ref: Cooper A and Waterworth T, Junior Education, July 1988)

Advantage: a variety of group activities which can be used to maximise a lack of equipment.

Disadvantage: children are introduced to one type of skill in each lesson.

(ii) All running, or all throwing, or all jumping activities eg:

Week		1	2	3	4	5	6
Introduction		Running activities	→	→	→	→	→
Skills (class)		Type of jumping 1──→1 1──→2 2──→2	Throwing overarm	Sprinting	Jumping combinations	Throwing push sling }	Running hurdling
Group activities (five groups)	1	2 ──→ 2	1 hand standing	40 m straight	A S W E E K 1	G R O U P shuttle R E L A Y S	Push large ball	Hurdle	G R O U P R E L A Y S	pass it on type
	2	3 steps	2 hands sitting	Zig-zag			Sling large ball	Potato shuttle		
	3	3 hops	1 hand run-up	40 m straight			Push bean bag	40 m straight		
	4	1 ──→ 2	2 hands sitting	Compass run			Sling quoit	Hurdle		
	5	3 of any combination	1 hand sling/bowl	Shape run 40 m			Push sitting 2 hands 1 hand	Zig-zag		

Advantage: group activities follow appropriate skill introduction.

Disadvantage: lack of variety in each session.

Each child should have a record book, a pencil, a marker (a bean bag) and a stopwatch to record their best performance.

Best! Activity	Week 1	Week 2	Week 3	Week 4	Week 5	Week 6
2 ──→ 2 standing jump	1.20 m					
3 steps						
Zig-zag run						

Group activity cards can be used to speed up and explain organisation of activities.

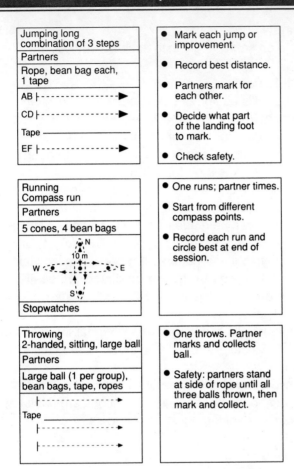

Jumping long combination of 3 steps	• Mark each jump or improvement.
Partners	• Record best distance.
Rope, bean bag each, 1 tape	• Partners mark for each other.
AB ⊢-------------►	• Decide what part of the landing foot to mark.
CD ⊢-------------►	
Tape ———————	
EF ⊢-------------►	• Check safety.

Running Compass run	• One runs; partner times.
Partners	• Start from different compass points.
5 cones, 4 bean bags	• Record each run and circle best at end of session.
Stopwatches	

Throwing 2-handed, sitting, large ball	• One throws. Partner marks and collects ball.
Partners	
Large ball (1 per group), bean bags, tape, ropes	• Safety: partners stand at side of rope until all three balls thrown, then mark and collect.
⊢-------------►	
Tape ——————	
⊢-------------►	
⊢-------------►	

It is also useful to devise a field/playground plan of activities to ensure that, for example, the throwing activities do not overlap, or running and turning points are not placed close to walls or windows.

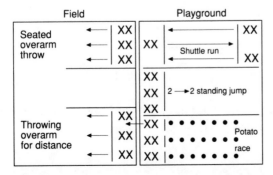

E. Safety
Advice on safety is given in each activity section.

F. Equipment
Games skills equipment can be used for key stage 2 athletic activities – no special equipment is necessary.
- Quoits can be used for all relay-type change-overs.
- Shots can be made from socks filled with bean bags.
- A quoit makes a perfect discus.
- An airflight ball fixed to the top of a cane makes a javelin, but follow throwing safety procedures.
- Hurdles can be made from skittles and garden canes or ropes weighted with bean-bags. The height can be adjusted to suit individuals (or groups of individuals). **Ensure that the hurdle can be dislodged easily.**
- Different size large balls are useful for throwing progressions.
- Airflight balls can be thrown with great force but travel small distances (hard balls cannot be used safely in class lessons).
- Playground chalk is useful for setting out.
- Ropes, bean bags, cones and hoops are useful as markers, for setting out and for targets.

G. Space
Some athletics skills can be taught and practised indoors, but are best taught outside where there is space to participate safely.

How to use the athletics activities section
Each set of activities represents a progressive scheme of work. Teachers can revisit activities (units of work) at different levels of difficulty with each year group.

Teaching points:
● Preparation for jumping: in a standing jump (no run up) the swinging of arms co-ordinated with the bending and springing from knees and ankles begins the action.
● Take-off: co-ordination of arm and leg action to propel the body into the air.
● Flight: keeping head and arms up as long as possible.
● Landing: safe, active, springy landing with rebound, especially on hard surfaces.
● Co-ordination: in take-off and between phases, as in a combination jump (eg, three steps).

Some parts of the skill can be presented as questions: 'How do you jump higher?' 'How can you jump further?', or illustrated by the use of contrasting tasks: 'Try jumping long without bending your knees/using your arms.'

Some skills have to be taught directly. Safe, springy landings are necessary on hard grass and playground surfaces. Warm-ups which include running and jumping can be used to remind pupils of the need and the skill of active landings.

Revise the four most appropriate jumping patterns:
● one foot to two feet (jump)
● one foot to the opposite foot (step)
● one foot to the same foot (hop)
● two feet to two feet (two-footed jump).

These are the basic actions for single and combination jumps and are best taught as introductory activities, eg: Using four grids, scatter ropes and hoops in the area:
● jog, stepping in and out of hoops or across ropes (one foot to the other);
● jog, jumping in and out of hoops or over ropes (one foot to two feet, two feet to two feet);
● jog, jump into hoop and out on same foot (one foot to the same foot).

1. Two feet to two feet jumping (standing start)
Teaching points:
● Preparation.
● Co-ordination: the timing of arm and leg actions and the height of the jump are instrumental in improving length.

Safety: encourage active landings which do not skid onto the seat (and which may jar the base of the spine).

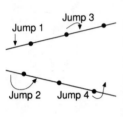

2. One foot to two feet jumping (standing start)
● One foot to two feet using a three-/five-stride approach. (a short approach is recommended to concentrate the effort on the jump). Measure the jump from the take-off to landing point. Encourage safe landings. Children can set out individual challenges using ropes and bean bags.

3. Combination jumping (standing start)
Teaching points:
●The landing phase of one jump merges with the preparation for the next jump. It is therefore important to keep the body upright on each landing to avoid a shorter jump on the next phase, and to keep the jumps of equal length. Set out ropes so that children can practice this co-ordination progressively.
● Ask children to find out how far they can jump using two or three steps; two or three hops; two or three two-footed jumps.
● Ask them to combine these techniques to find their best distance.

The pupils should jump over each rope, and can adjust the ropes to challenge themselves.

These combinations can be practised with three- or five-

4. Combination jumping (hop, step, jump sequence)
One to the same foot, to the opposite foot, to two-footed
landing). Children find the discipline of this sequence
challenging, and often revert to step, step, jump. Use
ropes at close intervals (see 3) to establish the basic
pattern.

5. Vertical jumping
A method of jumping high (a wall and some chalk are
needed). Pupils hold the chalk and mark their stretch
height on the wall, then jump and mark. The distance
between the two marks is their vertical jump height.

Safety: the landing phase is the biggest potential source
of injury, therefore no traditional high jumping is included
because of the lack of safe landing areas.

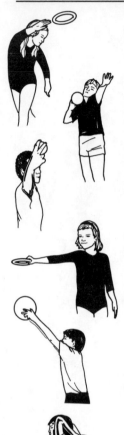

Teaching points:
● Body position/stance: a sideways stance is usual in all throwing, slinging, pushing actions.
● Transference of weight: from the rear foot to the front foot during the throwing action.
● Arm action: for overarm throwing, slinging, one-handed and two-handed pushing. The object being thrown is moving before it is released. The heavier the object, the more important it is to begin its movement in order to throw it a long way. Twisting the trunk in slinging and pushing aids the process of moving the object the furthest distance before it is released.
● Grip: for throwing, slinging and pushing.
● Force: the faster an action is performed, the longer the potential throw.
● Trajectory: the optimum release point to propel the object the furthest distance is at about 45° to the ground.

1. Underarm throwing for distance using a large ball
(a) facing forwards;
(b) facing backwards.
Which position allows you to move the ball the greatest distance before release? Answer: (b). Test your results.

2. Overarm throwing
(a) one-handed, standing, using a bean bag/airflight ball;
(b) one-handed with a three-/five-pace run up;
(c) two-handed, standing, with a large ball;
(d) as (c) with run-up.

3. Slinging
(a) two-handed using a large ball;
(b) one-handed using a quoit (forehand, straight-arm action);
(c) one-handed using a quoit-/frisbee-type grip/action.

Compare the distance of quoit throws. Which action produces the greatest distance?

Teaching points:
● Straight-arm action, one-handed. Encourage twisting the trunk to impart extra force to the quoit. Follow through with rear foot and arm in direction of throw. Children often bowl the quoit instead of slinging with a straight arm. Emphasise low start, high finish positions (45° trajectory).

4. Pushing
(a) two-handed sit, then stand;

Teaching points:
● Which position gives the longest throw? Why? (In a standing throw, use the trunk to give added leverage.)

(b) one-handed sit then stand using bean bag, bean bag sock or medium ball.

Teaching points:
● Sitting: concentrate on correct grip and pushing action. The elbow should be fixed and high, the object resting on the fingertips and fingers. The forearm moves. The palm faces the front all the time (a common fault is for the elbow to drop, resulting in throwing rather than pushing).
● Standing: concentrate on turning the trunk to start the object moving before release.

Safety: throw light equipment; throw into a free space; train your class to the following system:
● children spaced at least 2 m apart along a throwing line
● children work with a partner (A throws, B (non-thrower) collects. Change places)

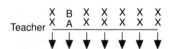

● all children throw at the same time
● all children collect after all throws have taken place.

Group throwing activities may need teacher supervision.

Teaching points:
- Arm action: for running fast;
  for running slowly.
- Leg action: speed of stride; length of stride.
- Acceleration: co-ordination of arms and legs; body position.

Sprinting progressions suitable for use with the whole class: introductory activities
- Jog on the spot, speeding up and slowing down stride rate.
- Jog on the spot, fast arms and legs with small strides. Move a short distance and repeat.
- Jog on the spot, speed up legs and practice pumping arms straight (not across chest).
- Jog on the spot with high knees.
- Stride on curving pathways with high knees; change to short fast strides; increase to striding.
- Sit on the ground. On signal, sprint for ten strides. What was the position of your body when you started? Leaning forward?

Teaching points:
- Running on the balls of the feet.
- Appropriate arm action for acceleration.
- 'Fast' legs – leg speed governs how fast you can go!
- Appropriate leaning body position for acceleration.

1. Set out six 30-m lanes using cones or bean bags (20 m for running, 10 m for slowing down). The first person in each lane runs, slows down in the safety area, turns and jogs back to their group down the outside of the track.

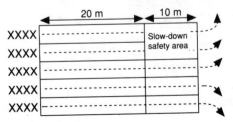

Teaching points:
- Use a start signal, eg 'Get-set, go'.
- Practice using the safety area and jogging back.
- Practice standing starts.
- Partner can place their feet to help grip, as with starting blocks.
- Increase sprint distance to 30 m for year 5 and 35 m for year 6.

2. Sprinting group activities

Shuttle

There and back 6 times = 60 m.
Adjust for age group, eg year 6 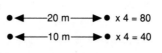 x 4 = 80
year 3 ● ◀—10 m—▶ ● x 4 = 40

Teaching points:
- Turning safety: touch the floor when turning.
- Acceleration after the turn: practice arm leg and body action; having touched the floor, the body is low.

3. Zig-zag/slalom

Practice running at speed on the curve, using short strides and body lean, then accelerate to finish.
Courses can be set out in a number of ways, eg:

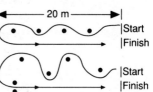

4. Compass run

Four runners can use the course starting at different compass points.

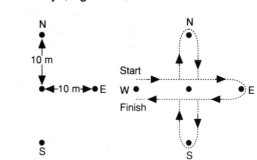

5. Shape run

What is the fastest method of getting round the course?

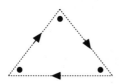

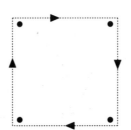

6. Hurdling
Class introduction progressions (groups of three or four).
(i) Place four ropes or cones on the ground and run over them as quickly as you can.

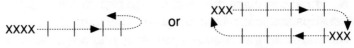

Teaching points:
● Establish which is the preferred take-off foot.

(ii) Run over the ropes taking off from the same foot each time. Pupils should find that they need an odd pattern of strides to enable them to take off on the same foot (three, five, seven, etc).

(iii) Adjust the ropes to three strides apart (children will have different stride lengths, depending on their leg length). Group the class for leg length. Practice again.

(iv) Introduce skittle and cane hurdles in place of ropes. Start at the lowest height and practice running fast over the hurdles. **Make sure the canes can be dislodged in the direction of the running.**

Raise the height and try to sprint (not jump) over the hurdles. What happens to the point of take-off? Will this increase the distance between hurdles?

(v) Increase the distance between each hurdle to five paces.

(vi) Use a group activity as a timed run: low hurdles to high hurdles; use a greater number of hurdles (adjust, as necessary, for individuals); sprinting in groups (relays).

7. Sprinting in groups – relays
Class progressions: introductory activities
(i) With a partner. One leading, one following, jog around the grid using curving pathways. When the leader puts their hand back, palm up, the follower taps it with their fingertips and jogs past to become the leader.

Teaching points:
● If the leader puts back the right hand, the follower taps the left hand and passes on the right. This teaches the correct relay passing technique. Vice-versa for left hand.

(ii) Same as (i) but the follower has a quoit, which they place with a downward action into the palm of the leader.
(iii) Same as (ii), but the leader opens their hand and the follower places the quoit with an upward action.

Skill development activities
● Running in a straight line in pairs.

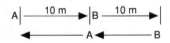

A has the quoit, runs to B and passes the quoit; B runs to the finish. Repeat, with B starting.

How can you change so that the receiver (B) is already moving? Answer: A calls 'Go' at the appropriate moment, or B places a marker on the track (eg, a bean bag).

Teaching points:
● A and B must change on the correct side (see (i)). The receiver must not look back for the quoit because this slows the changeover.
● Introduce a third person.

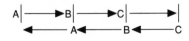

Practice changeovers there and back (pupils may find difficulty in deciding which side of the lane to stand to receive the quoit):

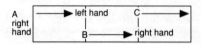

Relays: group activities

(i) As above.

● Introduce an element of competition: in groups of four run there-and-back relays. For older juniors, 25 m change-over distances are adequate.

(ii) Shuttle relays.

```
XCA|  ●          ● |BXX
xxx|  ●          ● |xxx
xxx|  ●          ● |xxx
```

● A runs with the quoit and places it on the cone. B picks it up, runs and places it on the cone, etc.

Safety: Cones are to prevent runners colliding during change-overs.

(iii) Team relays.

● For example: teams of six using a shuttle format.

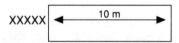

● Two pupils run there and back once = 40 m.
● Two pupils run there and back twice = 80 m.
● One pupil runs there and back three times = 60 m.
● One pupil runs there and back four times = 80 m.
● The team decides who runs which leg.

Athletics event

At the end of a unit of work an athletics team event can be organised to contextualise the skills practices. The mixed-ability groupings used for the group activities can be used to help design and organise the event.

Scoring: groups compete against each other.
Running events: the time for each runner is added to give a group time.
Jumping and throwing events: the distance of each jump/throw is added to give a group distance. The totals are the equivalent to a point score. Alternatively devise your own system.

1 Decide two running, two jumping and two throwing events.	3 Design entry form. Decide entries per group. Collate entries.
2 Every group member takes part in two different events minimum, plus group relay. Two entrants per event per group – all group in relay.	4 Discuss reasons for order of events. Design and produce a programme.

5 Decide organisation, eg rules/judging, recording, dress, safety, first-aid, event area, equipment, record sheets, absence, prizes, refreshments. Decide jobs.

6 Organise the event. Participate, judge, spectate.

7 Collate the results.

Event format ideas for running, jumping and throwing.

		Entrants	2 races (5 in each)	Judges		Record
R U N N I N G	Activity 1	10	1 2 3 4 5	1 2 3 4 5	Start 1 2	Finish 1 2	Record times on individual sheets.
	Activity 2	10	1 2 3 4 5	1 2 3 4 5	Start 1 2	Finish 1 2	

Final relay suggestion: 40 m shuttle type

One runner runs three legs = 120 m
Three runners run two legs = 240 m
One runner runs one leg   = 40 m
                            400 m

The group decides who runs which distance.

(Ref: Cooper A and Waterworth T, Junior Education, July 1988).